#9023

921 FOR

Richards, Kenneth G., 1926
Henry Ford,.

People of Destiny

A Humanities Series

There comes a time,
we know not when,
that marks
the destiny of men.

Joseph Addison Alexander

People of Destiny

HENRY FORD

By Kenneth Richards

For their cooperation in reviewing this manuscript the editors wish to express their appreciation to the members of the Ford Motor Company Educational Affairs Department

CHILDRENS PRESS, CHICAGO

The editors wish to express
their appreciation to Mr. Meyer Goldberg,
who created the series and inspired
the publication of People of Destiny

Cover and body design: John Hollis

Project editor: Joan Downing

Editorial assistant: Gerri Stoller

Illustrations: Bob Brunton, Nita Engle—
Hollis Associates

Research Editor: Robert Hendrickson

Photographs: From the files of Wide
World Photos, Inc., the Ford Archives,
and the Henry Ford Museum

Typesetting: Adcrafters Commercial
Typographers, Inc.

Printing: The Regensteiner Corporation

Quotations on pages 15; 16; 17; 19, col. 1, 11. 13-38; 20; 23, col. 1, 11. 32-34; 39; 47; 51; 54; 57; 59; 60; and 85 reprinted with the permission of Charles Scribner's Sons from FORD The Times, The Man, The Company, *by Allan Nevins and Frank Ernest Hill. Copyright 1954, Columbia University.*

Quotations on pages 62; 63; 64, col. 1, 11. 31-43; col. 2, 11. 1-2; 69; 77; 83; and 86 reprinted with the permission of Charles Scribner's Sons from FORD Expansion and Challenge, *by Allan Nevins and Frank Ernest Hill.*

Quotations on pages 10; 19, col. 1, 11. 45-48; 23, col. 1, 11. 39-42; and 27 reprinted with the permission of Mrs. Mary Owens Crowther from My Life and Work, *by Henry Ford and Samuel Crowther, Doubleday, Page & Co., 1923.*

Quotations on pages 23, col. 2, 11. 3-12; 64, col. 1, 11. 18-24 reprinted with the permission of Alfred A. Knopf from Henry Ford, *by Roger Burlingame.*

Library of Congress Catalog Card No. 67-20104

1 2 3 4 5 6 7 8 9 10 11 12 13 14 15 16 17 18 R 75 74 73 72 71 70 69 68 67

Contents

Triple Nine Pays Off

The crowd at Grosse Point racetrack pushed forward in anticipation as the roar of starting engines blasted the crisp autumn air. The date was October 25, 1902, and the Manufacturer's Challenge Cup Race was about to begin. Four of the fastest cars in America were entered in the five-mile event and the Detroit fans hoped to witness a new speed record. Perhaps one of the cars would average a miraculous mile-a-minute! The starting signal was given and the four roaring machines zoomed away in a billowing cloud of dust.

The race would be over in little more than five minutes, but the finish would mark the beginning of two new careers. The driver of the big red machine that jumped off to an early lead was Barney Oldfield. This was his first race, but henceforth his name would be synonymous with speed and daredevil driving. The man who had designed and built the big red "999" was Henry Ford. For him the end of the race would mark the beginning of a business career that would be unparalleled in the history of the United States. Within a few short years his

name would be a byword in every corner of the globe.

As Ford watched the cars roar past the starting line at the end of the first lap, he was little known outside his native Detroit. Oldfield held a considerable lead and it was plain that "999" was the fastest car on the course. Victory seemed to depend on Oldfield's performance and on the mechanical reliability of the car as it thundered into lap number two.

For Ford these were anxious moments as he watched his creation disappear down the track trailing a wispy cloud of smoke. He had staked his future plans and hopes on a victory this day. Since these plans required financial backing, he hoped to attract investors with the recognition a victory in the race would bring. Each turn of the crankshaft, each stroke of the cylinders of "999" brought that recognition closer to reality.

In the autumn of 1902, the "horseless carriage" was a steadily growing phenomenon of the American scene. To millions of Americans, however, the automobile was still little more than a name. But many more people were beginning to agree with Thomas Edison's remark, made in 1896, that "the horse is doomed!" The pioneers of the automobile age—Olds, Winton, Duryea, and others—were building cars at an ever-increasing rate, but they had barely scratched the surface of the vast potential market in America.

There were hazards involved in the new industry, however, and many companies failed after only a few months. Skilled technicians and machinists were hard to find. Production problems peculiar only to the manufacturing of automobiles had to be met and overcome—often by trial and error. Many cars were virtually handmade; the capability to mass-produce standard, interchangeable parts had not yet been fully developed. As many companies fell by the wayside, others learned from their experiences and prospered. Henry Ford had made two unsuccessful ventures into the automobile business. He had gained a great deal of experience and had an unshakable faith in his newly designed car. The blueprints for an even newer car were in his office. His dreams of the future hinged on "999's" performance that afternoon.

The cars roared past and began lap number three with Alexander Winton, the pre-race favorite, beginning to close the gap on Oldfield. The other two cars had fallen behind. It seemed to be a two-car race now, but could the big red machine keep up the pace?

The dream of Henry Ford was to build a reliable, standard automobile that the average man could afford. A "family horse" he called it. In this early age of the motorcar, most were available only to the very wealthy. A few moderately priced cars such as the Oldsmobile and the Pope-Tribune could be bought for under $1,000. Ford hoped to market a car for under $500. To do this he would have to build a great number of cars of one standard design. Most manufacturers offered a selection varying widely in design and cost. Many were building cars to order. Ford reasoned that it would cost less to build a single style and type of automobile. He would pass this saving on to the customer.

As Ford himself expressed it, "I will build a motor car for the great multitude. It will be large enough for the family but small enough for the individual to run and care for. It will be constructed of the best materials, by the best men to be hired, after the simplest design that modern engineering can devise. But it will be so low in price that no man making a good salary will be unable to own one —and enjoy with his family the blessing of hours of pleasure in God's great open spaces." The rich enjoyment that we take so much for granted in this day and age was, at the turn of the century, only a dream and a vision in the mind of Henry Ford.

As the "999" roared into the final lap, Ford noted that Winton had dropped out of the race. His car could not stand the pace set by Oldfield, who never thought of letting up in the

Henry Ford was not the first man to build an automobile in the United States. The pioneers of the automobile age—Olds, Winton, Duryea, and others—were building cars at an ever-increasing rate by 1902. Shown here, from top to bottom, are an 1893 Duryea, a 1900 Winton Motor Carriage, a 1902 Olds, and a 1903 Packard.

turns. Even with his only real competitor now out of the race, daredevil Barney continued to thunder around the track at full tilt. He had passed one of the other cars in lap four and now as he rumbled into the final stretch he passed the other to cross the finish line more than a mile ahead of his closest rival.

The joyous hometown fans spilled onto the track in a cheering mass to welcome the victor. Barney Oldfield, wind-frayed cigar clenched in his teeth, had won his first race. He had completed the course in 5:28 minutes —just a little over 57 miles per hour —to set a new American record.

Henry Ford's gamble paid off. The victory brought him national recognition. In the coming weeks, he and his associates began to seek out investors —always pointing with pride to the victory at Grosse Point. The high mortality rate of automobile companies had caused among investors a growing reluctance to place their money with such a risky undertaking. But many apparently reasoned that any man who could design a car as powerful and reliable as "999" would

be a fairly safe bet to succeed with a commercial automobile.

At last sufficient backing was obtained and on June 16, 1903, the Ford Motor Company was incorporated. By the first anniversary of the victory of "999," the new career of Henry Ford was firmly launched on its meteoric ride. In the years to come his dreams, his ambitions, and his talents would have an increasing impact on the lives of every American. His life's work, from this time forward, would help reshape the destiny of America.

Joyous Detroit fans spill onto the track at Grosse Point, Michigan, to welcome racing driver Barney Oldfield (inset, top), who had just driven to victory in the Manufacturer's Challenge Cup Race on October 25, 1902. This was Oldfield's first race, but henceforth his name would be synonymous with speed and daredevil driving. The car he drove was the "999," designed and built by Henry Ford (inset, bottom). Oldfield's victory at Grosse Point brought Ford national recognition and sufficient financial backing to incorporate the Ford Motor Company by June, 1903.

The Tinkering Farm Boy

The guns of Gettysburg had been silent less than a month when Henry Ford was born near the little community of Dearborn, Michigan, on July 30, 1863. He would be nearly two years old before the Civil War ended, but the quiet rural area of southern Michigan was never to know the horrors of war. The first son of William and Mary Ford was born into a world of peace and pleasant surroundings.

Contrary to many stories and legends, Henry Ford was not raised in a log cabin. His birthplace, which he later restored, was a comfortable farmhouse—in fact a rather large one for the area. The eleven-room house and several outbuildings were surrounded by ninety-one acres of rich farm and timberland. There was also a truck garden and a well-stocked orchard. Young Henry was never to want for food or warm clothing—though most of the clothing was handmade.

His father, William Ford, was born in Cork, Ireland, and came to America with his parents in 1847. Other Fords, in the 1830's, had been among the pioneers who carved a little settlement in the virgin Michigan land. No doubt the letters home to Ireland, telling of the wonders of the New

Henry Ford's mother, Mary Litogot Ford (above), came from a hard-working Pennsylvania Dutch family. She was a "dark-haired, dark-eyed young woman with a hint of a smile." His father, William (above, right), was born in Cork, Ireland, and came to America with his parents in 1847.

World, prompted William's family to emigrate. William, then a teen-ager, shared with his parents the dreams of a new land and prosperity.

Arriving in Dearborn, the family was probably distributed among the relatives until land could be purchased and a home built. In January of 1848, the family purchased eighty acres of land, built a house, and settled down to begin life on the Michigan frontier.

William helped his parents clear the land and work the soil. Until a sufficient area could be cleared for crops, the family lived on what cash could be realized from the trees, which were cut into cordwood and timber. William also worked for several years for the Michigan Central Railroad as a carpenter.

About 1850, William began working for Patrick O'Hern, a fairly well-to-do farmer in Dearborn. The O'Herns had a ten-year-old adopted daughter, Mary Litogot, whose parents had died when she was quite young. Through the years William watched her grow to womanhood and in 1861, when Mary was twenty-one and he thirty-five, they were married. Soon after the wedding, the newlyweds moved in with the O'Herns. The couples enjoyed a close family relationship from the very first. Patrick and William immediately set to work building a new and larger house that was to be the childhood home of Henry Ford.

William Ford had a deep love for the land. A hard-working pioneer, who cleared and cultivated the land he owned, he has been described as a "moderately successful farmer." He never accumulated great wealth but was always able to provide well for his family. His farm was nearly self-sufficient, with a sawmill, a gristmill, and machinery for making wool sheared from the sheep he raised.

From a very early age, Henry took a dislike for manual farm work. As he was to state later, "I have followed many a weary mile behind a plough and I know the drudgery of it." From the very first he tended to avoid all the chores that normally fell to a farm boy on the frontier. He was not lazy, but his interest—his mother said he was "born with it"—lay with things mechanical. He was sure, from his earliest youth, that machines could be built to reduce the back-breaking toil of the farmer.

If William Ford was unable to influence Henry to farm life, he nonetheless passed on many virtues to his eldest son. From his father the future industrialist inherited a diligence to see a job done well. William Ford had the self-reliance so necessary to life on the frontier. William's rigid moral values were equally important in the development of Henry Ford. His later devotion to family and home bore the mark of the close family relationship he had enjoyed in his youth.

While his father could never understand Henry's dislike of farm work, his mother encouraged his interest in mechanics. In fact, she exerted a greater influence on his life and work than any other individual. In later years he would say, "I have tried to live my life as my mother would have wished. I believe I have done, as far as I could, just what she hoped of me."

Mary Litogot Ford has been described as a "dark-haired, dark-eyed young woman with a hint of a smile, and an air of earnestness and integrity." Her family were Pennsylvania Dutch, all hard-working, thrifty people with a love and talent for the soil. She was a cheerful, understanding woman who met the many tasks required of a farmer's wife with competence and self-assurance. In later years, Henry was to remember that his mother dominated the home. "She presided over it and ruled it," he said, "She made it a good place to be."

She was a firm disciplinarian but never resorted to corporal punishment. Once, caught in a lie, Henry was to recall later that, "mother made me suffer the experience of a liar. For a day I was treated with contempt and I knew that I had done a despicable thing . . . I learned from her that wrong-doing carries its own punishment. There is no escape."

Mary instilled in her children a deep sense of obligation. "Fun we had and plenty of it," Henry was to recall, "but she was forever reminding us that life cannot be all fun. 'You must earn the right to play,' she used to say to me. One of her sayings used to be, 'The best fun follows a duty done.' " Whenever young Henry found a particular chore disagreeable, she would remind him that such jobs call for " 'courage and patience and self-discipline,' and she taught me also that 'I don't want to' gets a fellow nowhere . . . My mother used to say, when I grumbled about it, 'life will give you many unpleasant tasks to do; your duty will be hard and disagreeable and painful to you at times, but you must do it. You may have pity on others but you must not pity yourself. Do what you know you must do to the best of your ability.' "

Henry's aversion to war and his pacifism of later years were probably,

". . . she was forever reminding us that life cannot be all fun . . . . The best fun follows a duty done."

to a large extent, inherited from his mother. Eight months before his birth she had lost a brother in the battle of Fredericksburg. Then, just a month before Henry was born, another brother was badly wounded at Gettysburg. No doubt, too, her feelings about things military were derived partly from her stepfather, Patrick O'Hern, who had deserted from the British army while stationed in Canada. Apparently the Ford side of the family, also, had an aversion to military service. Of all the Fords living in Dearborn, not one volunteered for military service during the Civil War. As will be seen, however, when America became involved in World Wars I and II, Henry Ford would turn the mighty capacity of his plants totally to the war effort.

Mary Ford, who had been a good student, taught her eldest son to read. Henry once wrote in a diary, "Could read all the first readers before I started school. My mother taught me." In addition, she passed on to her children traditional religious and social values. She taught them that they should not drink, smoke, or gamble. Henry remained faithful to these principles all his life. Mother and father alike imbued in the children a firm sense of duty.

Henry was not yet thirteen when his mother died in childbirth. By now he had four brothers and a sister. The family was overwhelmed with grief. As Henry was to say later, "the house was like a watch without a mainspring." For awhile an aunt and an older cousin came to manage the household, but in time his younger sister Margaret assumed the task. Within a year disaster struck again when his youngest brother also died. But with the will and strength inherited from their mother, the little family carried on.

Thus, at a very formative period, Henry Ford was suddenly deprived of the most important guiding influence of his life. William, though a kind and loving father, could never understand his son's aversion to farm life. The boy missed the mother who had appreciated and encouraged his interest in machines. Henry disliked horses and loathed even the smell of cows. Nothing his father could do would change him.

With no one left to turn to for real understanding, Henry Ford's traits of independence and self-sufficiency were strengthened. His father's character, no doubt, had a stabilizing influence on the boy. His example of duty and hard work must have affected his son, despite Henry's distaste for farming. But years later Henry was to say, "I never had any particular love for the farm. It was the mother on the farm I loved."

And so, by 1876—the year of "Custer's Last Stand"—the basic character of Henry Ford had been formed. The teachings of his mother and the examples set by his father had instilled in the boy a set of values he would carry all his life.

No Plows for Henry

It was not long after his mother's death that Henry Ford saw a self-propelled road vehicle for the first time. One day in July, just before his thirteenth birthday, he and his father were driving a team of horses when they met a steam engine moving along the road under its own power. This event, probably one of the most important of his life, is best told in his own words.

Nearly a half-century later he was to say, "I remember that engine as though I had seen it only yesterday. The engine had stopped to let us pass with our horses and I was off the wagon and talking to the engineer before my father, who was driving, knew what I was up to. It was intended primarily for driving threshing machines and sawmills and was simply a portable engine and boiler mounted on wheels with a water tank and a coal cart trailing behind. I had seen plenty of these engines hauled around by horses, but this one had a chain that made a connection from the propelling wheel and a belt put on to drive other machinery. He told me that the chain pinion could be shifted to let the wagon stop while the engine was still running. This last is a feature which, although in different fashion, is incorporated into modern automotive transportation."

The incident, Ford said later, "showed me that I was by instinct an engineer." Thus a spark was struck that was to fire the imagination of Henry Ford for years to come.

While this was Henry's first encounter with self-propulsion, his childhood up to that time had demonstrated an ever-growing interest in mechanical things. He once said, "I always had a pocketful of trinkets, nuts and washers and odds and ends of machinery." As a boy he could be found wherever there was a machine —watching the threshers, sharpening the saws in the sawmill, mending broken plows, hoes, mowers, and reapers. He frequently rode around the countryside in search of such things to fix and, much to his father's chagrin, never accepted any money for his efforts.

Except for his mechanical bent, his childhood was typical of that of other boys who grew up in Michigan rural communities of the period. He first entered school in January of 1871, when he was seven and a half years old. The Scotch Settlement School, which he first attended, was about a mile and a half from his home; Henry walked the distance each morning and evening. The school was a little red brick building with one large room, a wood stove, double wooden desks, and a "bad boys bench." The basic "three R's" were taught in the little school and there were courses in geography, mental arithmetic, and general science for the older students. Henry's favorite subject throughout his school life was arithmetic; he was least happy with literature—especially fiction.

His best pal, for whom he would later name his only son, was Edsel Ruddiman. Both were lively boys, often given to mischief-making, and the two spent quite a few hours on the "mourner's bench" directly under the eye of the teacher. They once devised a sort of code with which to write notes that the teacher could not decipher.

As Henry grew older, his mechanical curiosity and aptitude grew with him. He was a natural leader and other boys followed him willingly in his schemes and experiments. Once Henry and his busy band decided to build a dam across a little creek that ran near the school. Working throughout the noon recess, they soon had their dam—complete with a crude waterwheel. When the school bell called them back to class, they left the dam standing. That night a heavy rain caused the stream to overflow into a farmer's potato patch. Next day, when

---

Just before his thirteenth birthday, Henry Ford saw a self-propelled road vehicle (opposite) for the first time. The "portable engine and boiler mounted on wheels with a water tank and a coal cart trailing behind" struck a spark that was to fire the imagination of Henry Ford for years to come.

the furious farmer confronted the schoolteacher, the young engineers were ordered to tear out the dam.

The dam experiment was only one of many concocted in the fertile mind of the future industrialist. Another time he and his schoolmates constructed a "steam turbine" which they set up against the school fence. Though it developed little power, they did manage to get 3000 rpm's out of the engine before it suddenly blew up in their faces. Ford noted that it "blew a piece through my lip and a piece hit Robert Blake in the abdomen and put him OUT!" While none of the personal injuries were serious, the explosion set fire to the school fence. Henry's father repaired the fence, and though he did not scold or punish the boy, he quietly pointed out the hazards of being careless while working with machinery.

On another occasion, Henry built a forge in a shed near the school. Soon the boys had rigged up a blower and were busy melting glass and recasting it in various shapes. His tinkerings, however, were not limited to the school yard. Anything mechanical had to be explored. It got so that when a new toy came into the Ford home, someone would yell, "Don't let Henry see it! He'll take it apart!"

As the boy grew older, he had to assume more and more of the many chores associated with farm life. On all the farms in the community there were animals to be cared for; crops to be sown, tended, and harvested; trees to be felled and cut into cordwood, carried home and cut into stovelength; and a hundred other sundry tasks so necessary to sustaining a family. These were the tasks Henry

---

As Henry Ford grew older, he had to assume more and more of the many chores associated with farm life. There were animals to be cared for (opposite); crops to be sown, tended, and harvested (left); trees to be felled and cut into cordwood, carried home and cut into stovelength; and a hundred other sundry tasks so necessary to sustaining a family—tasks that Henry so disliked.

"DEARBORN"
Public School

so disliked. But there were also jobs of maintaining the equipment and repairing the tools. The young mechanic thrived on these tasks. The Ford equipment was kept in better condition than that on any other farm in the area.

But life was not all schoolwork and chores. There were grand and wonderful times to be had when the chores were done. The surrounding forests abounded with wild game. Partridge, rabbits, foxes, raccoons, and mink all lived in the nearby woods. The Roulo Creek and, a little farther away, the Rouge River, provided excellent fishing.

There were also the many delightful hours of swimming in the old swimming hole, kite flying in the first gusty breezes of spring, and a dozen children's games when the gang could get together. Games like "mumbley peg," "crack the whip," "prisoner's base," "One-O-Cat," and "ante-ante-over" were popular pastimes for Henry and his pals. Yet, Henry often seemed happiest when he could find a machine or tool to work with.

In his bedroom he built a workbench. He was later to say that he had this ". . . workshop, with odds and ends for tools before I had anything else." On his thirteenth birthday he received a watch—his very own to do with as he pleased. He promptly took it apart and put it back together again. He had soon mastered the mechanics of a watch and later said "by the time I was fifteen I could do almost anything in watch repairing, although my tools were of the crudest." His reputation as a watch repairman grew and before long he was repairing clocks and watches for the whole community. One day a group of his pals brought him a watch that they had taken completely apart. "Come on Henry, let's see if you can put this together," they said. To their astonishment, in half an hour he had assembled all the parts into a perfectly running timepiece.

"Machines are to a mechanic what books are to a writer," Henry liked to say. "A real mechanic ought to know how nearly everything is made. He gets ideas from them and if he has any brains he will apply those ideas." One biographer said of Ford, "From the earliest time he was a master of mechanical logic: from a glance at any machine he could understand the interdependence of its parts—follow a line of reasoning, however long, through gears, ratchets, spurs, cams, and levers. . . . It was never his habit to write things down. He fitted details into a logical train of thought."

In the three years following his mother's death, Henry matured into young manhood. As his share of the farm work increased, so did his independence. He attended the county fairs and the circus, sometimes with his family and sometimes with his pals. There were skating parties and church social activities to liven the hours when the farm work was done and he often made trips into Detroit, some ten miles away.

As he reached his sixteenth birthday, he was becoming more and more dissatisfied with life on the farm. With each trip to the city, he became increasingly drawn to the factories and machine shops with their wonderful tools and humming machines. At last the attraction became too great and he made the decision to leave the farm and strike out on his own.

After talking things over with his father, who made no objection, Henry Ford left the farm on December 1, 1879, and went to Detroit. He walked all the way, and with less than five dollars in his pocket stepped into a new and exciting world of machines and engines. Another quarter-century would pass before his name would be known across the length and breadth of America. But on this cold December day the spark that would kindle the flame of industrial revolution smoldered in the mind of Henry Ford.

On the opposite page are shown (top) the schoolhouse in Dearborn, Michigan, that Henry Ford attended as a boy and (bottom) the Ford home in which Henry was born.

“Keep At It, Young Man”

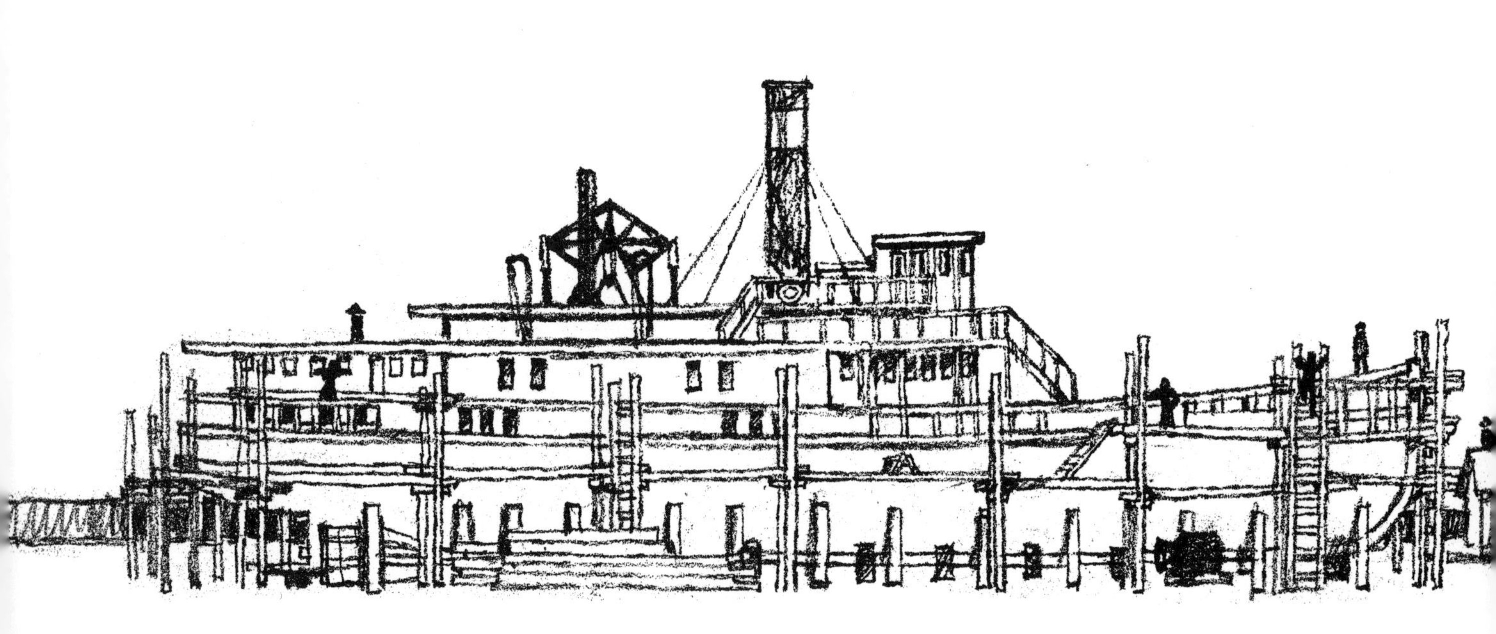

Ford's first job in Detroit lasted only six days. No one knows the exact reason, but there are several stories concerning his brief stay. All seem to agree, though, that the eager young man quickly antagonized the older men with his intuitive ability to solve mechanical problems. Whatever the reason, he was without a job only briefly, for he found employment with friends of his father who owned the James Flower and Brothers Machine Shop.

Henry began his apprenticeship at the plant with a weekly wage of $2.50. Since his room and board came to $3.50 per week, it was necessary for him to find a part-time job. He soon learned that a jeweler, just a few doors from his boardinghouse, needed a watch repairman. He quickly convinced the jeweler of his ability and was hired to work nights at $2.00 per week. He now had a dollar per week left over after paying for his room and board. At the jeweler's shop, Henry was forced to work out of sight at a bench in the back room. The jeweler felt that customers would not want to entrust their valuable timepieces to such a young boy.

After nine months with the Flower Brothers, during which time he received a raise to $3.00 a week, Henry changed jobs once again. Feeling that he had learned all he could in the machine shop, he took a job as a machinist's apprentice with the Detroit Drydock Company. This company was the largest of Detroit's shipbuilding firms. Young Ford was employed in the engine works. Here he had the opportunity to gain first-hand experience with many types and sizes of power plants. By 1882, he had completed his three-year apprenticeship and became a full-fledged journeyman. He was making $5.00 a week and could afford to give up his part-time job at the jewelers. By the mid-eighties, however, he felt that he could learn no more in his present position and decided to leave.

His next job was selling portable steam engines as a local representative of the Westinghouse Company. As an expert in installation and repair, Ford traveled around southern Michigan, going to farm houses to install engines and show the farmers how to operate them. Recalling his chores on the farm, he devoted much thought

Henry Ford left his father's farm in 1879 and went to Detroit. He worked at the James Flowers and Brothers Machine Shop for about nine months and then took a job as a machinist's apprentice with the Detroit Drydock Company (below). This company was the largest of Detroit's shipbuilding firms. Ford, employed in the engine works, had the opportunity to gain first-hand experience with many types and sizes of power plants. By 1882, he had completed his three-year apprenticeship and became a full-fledged journeyman.

to the invention of a machine that would relieve the farmer of his back-breaking toil. He was later to write of this period, "I kept experimenting with various sorts of boilers. I knew there was no difficulty in designing a big tractor for use on a large farm, but the manufacturing of a big tractor which only a few wealthy farmers could buy did not seem to me worthwhile." Even at that time he believed that no product designed especially for a select market would ever be worthwhile.

Henry had several other jobs in the mid eighteen-eighties, and also spent a good share of his time back on his father's farm. For awhile he attended the Goldsmith, Bryant and Stratton Business University in Detroit which taught bookkeeping, business transactions, and typewriting.

Life for young Henry, then in his early twenties, was not all machines and farming. He and his pals went skating, riding, and sleighing and often attended parties in the homes of friends and neighbors. He did his share of dating, too, and it was during this period that he learned to dance. One night during the winter of 1885 he was introduced to an attractive, dark-haired girl by the name of Clara Bryant. They were attracted to each other from the very beginning. Their courtship was to last for over three years. They were married on April 11, 1888.

During the winter of 1885 Henry Ford was introduced to an attractive, dark-haired girl by the name of Clara Bryant (opposite). After a three-year courtship, they were married in 1888. He and his wife often went sleighing (left) and attended parties in the homes of friends and neighbors.

Meanwhile, in late 1886, William Ford offered his son eighty acres of land not far from Henry's childhood home. Henry accepted the land, but had no thought of giving up his tinkering with machinery. Soon after his marriage, he built and equipped a workshop not far from the rude little dwelling that was their first home. Henry never did any serious farming, though he did cultivate a small amount of cleared land. The sawmill that he ran and occasional engine-repair jobs in Detroit were his chief sources of income. Still, the couple prospered, and after a year moved into a larger, more attractive home they had built on the property.

It was here that Ford first began talking about a "horseless carriage." He had heard of self-propelled vehicles then being developed both in this country and abroad. For awhile he experimented with a steam engine that he bolted to the bottom of a buggy. It actually ran for about four car lengths—and then stopped. There was one insurmountable problem—he could not come up with a satisfactory boiler for a lightweight vehicle.

One night in the late summer of 1891, Ford came home from a repair job in Detroit with an idea. He had been working with an Otto internal-combustion engine and was convinced that this type of engine was the answer to building a horseless carriage.

After sketching his proposed invention for his wife, he went on to say that in order to develop his idea successfully he would need to know more about electricity. His next statement was a shocker for Clara. He had inquired at the Edison Illuminating Company about a job and wanted to leave the farm and move to the city! Clara confessed years later that it nearly broke her heart to leave the farm. But she had confidence in her husband's ability and she quietly agreed to make the move.

Henry was then twenty-eight years old. He was giving up a great measure of security on the farm to begin a new life in the city. If his ideas were still vague and his goal still indefinite, at least he was back with his beloved ma-

chines, working once again where he was happiest.

Ford was highly regarded at Edison and advanced rapidly, becoming chief engineer in 1893. In November of that year he became a father for the first and only time. His son Edsel arrived on the sixth of that month.

In the meantime, Henry labored evenings and weekends on his engine —a simple and experimental thing. On Christmas Eve in 1893, he brought the engine into the house and mounted it on the kitchen sink so he could use the house electrical current for his spark plug. Clara was appalled, but after a little coaxing she assisted her husband in getting the little engine to run. After a few moments of gratifying noise and vibration, Ford let the motor die and then took it back out to the garage to proceed to his next step. "I didn't stop to play with it," he said years later.

The idea of a gasoline-powered motor vehicle was not a novel one. Though lagging somewhat behind European inventors, the first American automobile ran in public in September, 1883. It had been built and driven by the Duryea brothers near Springfield, Massachusetts. Elwood Haynes had run his car for the first time on July 4, 1894. Ransom Olds, Percy Maxim, and others were working busily on their own models. The first American automobile race was run in Illinois on Thanksgiving Day, 1895, with a top prize of $2000. The race, run in a foot of snow, was from the south side of Chicago to Evanston and back—a distance of about fifty miles. Frank Duryea won the contest with an average running time of about six and one-half miles per hour.

Meanwhile, Ford was making good progress with his little car. As it neared completion, Ford hardly slept at all. Clara was beginning to be con-

The first American automobile race was run in Illinois on Thanksgiving Day, 1895. The race—from the south side of Chicago to Evanston and back—was won by Frank Duryea (left) with an average running time of about six and one-half miles per hour.

On June 4, 1896, Henry Ford's first car—his dream car—was finished. It weighed only 500 pounds and was the lightest vehicle of its type yet produced. At left, thirty-three-year-old Henry, wearing his Sunday best and a jaunty mustache, sits in his "quadricycle." The car, powered by a two-cylinder, four-cycle engine, had an electric bell in front to warn pedestrians.

cerned for his health, but she kept her worries to herself. Finally, at two o'clock on the morning of June 4, 1896, Henry's dream car was finished.

The car, weighing only 500 pounds, was the lightest vehicle of its type yet produced. Made almost entirely of wood, (except of course the motor, axles, wheels, etc.), it ran on four bicycle-type wheels with pneumatic tires. It was steered with a handle and the seat was a bicycle saddle. It was driven by a chain drive and featured a compensating gear to equalize the power applied to the rear wheels when turning a corner. It had no reverse gear so it could move only forward.

Despite the fact that it was raining on that June morning in 1896, Ford and Jim Bishop, his friend and helper, decided to make a trial run. Then, to his dismay, Ford found that the garage doors were too small to accommodate the car! Not to be deterred, Ford seized an ax and knocked out enough of the brick wall to permit his car to pass. With Bishop riding ahead on a bicycle to warn horse-drawn vehicles, Ford edged his little "quadricycle" out over the cobblestone streets. His moment of triumph had arrived. After a short run through the darkened streets, attracting a small group of amazed spectators even at this hour, the two happy men returned home for a few winks of sleep.

In the coming weeks Ford rebuilt his car, strengthened it with steel, installed a seat large enough for himself and a passenger, and added a cooling system to the motor. He and his friends or Clara would often go driving around Detroit, causing quite a sensation wherever they went. One day Henry, Clara, and baby Edsel took a drive out to the old home at Dearborn. Henry's father examined the car and listened to his son's explanation of how it worked, but could not be persuaded to go for a ride.

Wherever they went, bicyclists would chase after the car, and wherever it stopped, a crowd would gather. Ford later recalled, "If I stopped my machine anywhere, a crowd was around it before I could start it up again. If I left it alone for even a minute some inquisitive person always tried to run it. Finally, I had to carry a chain and chain it to a lamppost whenever I left it anywhere."

In August, Ford was sent to New York as a delegate to an Edison convention. There he had the great good fortune to meet Thomas Edison himself. Seated together at a banquet, Edison asked Ford questions about his horseless carriage. Henry drew some sketches for him on the back of a menu. Edison was enthusiastic and finally said, "Young man, that's the thing! You have it—the self-contained unit carrying its own fuel with it! Keep at it!"

Such encouragement from the great "Wizard of Menlo Park" filled Ford with new inspiration. A short time later, Ford sold his little car for $200 and immediately began building a second. "I was looking ahead to production," he was to recall, "but before that could come I had to have something to produce." His greater plan for the future was already beginning to take shape in his mind.

By the summer of 1899, Ford had completed his second car. In the two and one-half years since the sale of his first car, Henry had invested all his spare time and money in the development of the new car—and his natural leadership talents had enabled him to find both assistants and backers for the enterprise. His faith and confidence in his plans were contagious and his friends and acquaintances found themselves caught up in his enthusiasm.

The new car was a more substantial machine than the first had been. It weighed about 875 pounds, had larger wheels and tires, and an upholstered seat. Though it had a more finished look than its predecessor, it retained the "buggy" lines so common to the early automobiles. In his latest car, Ford had done away with the chain drive and used a gear-type transmission. The new model also featured two forward speeds and one reverse. The car ran satisfactorily and, after a few demonstration runs, Ford succeeded in interesting enough backers to form his first company.

Ford had decided that in order to develop his horseless-carriage engine successfully he would need to know more than he did about electricity. He obtained a job at the Edison Illuminating Company in 1891, and by 1893 had been promoted to chief engineer. In August of 1896, two months after he had finished building his first car, he was sent to New York as a delegate to an Edison convention. There he showed the enthusiastic Thomas Edison (left) some sketches of the horseless carriage.

The Detroit Automobile Company, as it was called, was formed on August 5, 1899, and on August 15, Ford resigned from the Edison firm where he had worked for eight years. He became superintendent and a small stockholder in the new company and enthusiastically turned to the production of his first commercial car. Early in 1900, his first model was ready for public display.

The first car was built as a delivery wagon to stress the practical applications of the automobile. In February, Ford took a reporter from the Detroit *News-Tribune* for a ride—probably the reporter's first—and the article written by the ecstatic journalist demonstrates the reaction most men would have felt about this new phenomenon.

"With incomparable swiftness," he reported, "the automobile flew over the icy streets." As he was rushed along at twenty to twenty-five miles per hour, the reporter was impressed with a new noise in history—the noise of the automobile. "It was not like any other sound ever heard in this world," he said. "A long, quick, mellow gurgling sound, not harsh, not unmusical, not distressing; a note that falls with pleasure on the ear. It must be heard to be appreciated. And the sooner you hear its newest chuck! chuck! the sooner you will be in touch with civilization's latest lisp, its newest voice." As they passed a harness shop, Ford cried, "His trade is doomed!" "The horse is doomed!" echoed his passenger, and the automobile "slipped like a sunbeam around the corner."

Despite the obvious rapture of the reporter, the Detroit Automobile Company ground slowly out of business during the first year of the new century. The car they were making was simply too expensive. In November, the company closed its doors and once more Henry Ford was looking for a new approach into the budding new industry.

Early in 1901, the year President McKinley was assassinated, Ford began thinking of racing as a means of attracting public recognition. Soon he was hard at work building a racing car. "The public refused to consider the automobile in any light other than a fast toy."

On October 10, Ford entered his car in a race held at Grosse Point—scene of his later triumph with "999." Driving his new 26-horsepower racer himself, he beat his only competitor, Alexander Winton, and won the race amid the cheers of the hometown crowd. As a result of this victory, Ford attracted new backers. In November, the ever-enthusiastic inventor was back in business as an engineer and stockholder of the Henry Ford Company. Almost from the beginning, however, dissension developed between Ford and other stockholders. In March of 1902, he left the company with $900 and the uncompleted drawings for a racing car. The company also agreed to discontinue use of his name.

In the meantime, Ford had made the acquaintance of Tom Cooper, a former bicycle-racing champion who had quite a bit of money and a real interest in automobile racing. Cooper offered to back Ford in the development of a racing car. About this time Ford met another young man who would figure prominently in Ford enterprises in the years ahead. He was C. Harold Wills, an engineer who shared the dreams and visions Henry Ford had for the automobile industry. In the early spring of 1902, they worked together untiringly in the unheated second-story workshop that Ford had rented. There is a story that when they became too chilled to work they would put on a pair of boxing gloves and spar a few rounds until they were warm.

By late summer they had completed two racers, the "Arrow" and "999." The latter car, their big hope, was low slung and, for that early age of the automobile, powerful and rakish in design. The motor, completely exposed, belched flames from its four seven-inch cylinders. As Ford said, "The roar of those cylinders alone was enough to half kill a man!" Like Ford's first two cars, this one also was steered by a heavy iron bar or "steering handle." It was, indeed, an awesome brute for its day, but daredevil Barney Oldfield was not afraid of it and, as we have read, he piloted the big machine to victory.

The victory and resulting recognition launched Henry Ford on a new career with greater opportunity and promise than ever before. He formed the Ford Motor Company. It would prove to be the major turning point in his life.

Pictured on the opposite page are Henry Ford (standing) and Barney Oldfield with the low-slung, powerful racing car, "999."

"The roar of those cylinders alone was enough to half kill a man!"

Through the Alphabet

The Ford Motor Company, as formed in June of 1903, issued 1000 shares of stock valued nominally at $100 per share. Actually, of the $100,000 represented, only $28,000 was in cash.

Even before the victory of "999," Ford had formed a partnership with A. Y. Malcomson, a moderately wealthy coal dealer. For Malcomson, the venture was something of a gamble and for awhile he did not want to commit himself too heavily. After the victory at Grosse Point, however, he decided to invest more money in the business. Both he and Ford now received 255 shares of stock in the new company. These shares represented work done previously in developing a model car, plans, machinery, and patents. John Gray, a banker and Malcomson's uncle, was the largest cash investor with 105 shares representing $10,500. He was elected president; Ford, vice-president; Malcomson, treasurer; and James Couzens, secretary. At a directors meeting soon after the company was formed, Ford was assigned a salary of $3600 per year.

With so little capital to work with, the company was forced to build and sell as rapidly as possible before the bills from the parts makers fell due. At one point in early July, the com-

Ford's first Model A car (shown above) was a "runabout," which weighed about 1250 pounds and was powered by a two-cylinder engine. The car could run at speeds up to thirty miles per hour. It had no door, no running board, and only a six-foot wheelbase. At extra cost, a "tonneau"—a detachable rear seat—was available to the customer.

pany had a balance of only a little over $200—and not a car had yet been sold! Then, just when disaster seemed about to strike, a check for $850 arrived from a Dr. Pfennig—the first man to buy a car from the Ford Motor Company—and the race against the bill collector was won. During the next few days, other orders came in and soon the trickle of payments grew to a steady stream. In late August, the company showed a balance of over $23,000. It had been close, but now the Ford Motor Company was off to a flying start.

The first building occupied by the firm was an old wagon shop on Mack Avenue in Detroit. It was renovated for use as an automobile assembly plant. In these early days of the industry, no company manufactured all its own parts. Contracts were let to many different builders and final assembly of the component parts was done at a central plant. Thus, the various parts of Ford's cars were built in scattered firms around the city and transported (by horse-drawn conveyance) to the Mack Avenue plant.

The engines, of Ford's design, were manufactured in Detroit by the Dodge brothers, as were the axles and transmissions. These parts, the so-called "running gear," cost Ford $250 each. The wooden bodies from the Wilson Carriage Company cost $52 each and the cushions $16. The wheels, made in Lansing, cost $26 per set, and the tires from the Hartford Rubber Company were $10 apiece. Thus the basic parts of Ford's automobile came to $384. When the cost of assembling these parts, plus the cost of sales and advertising, were added, the total cost of the car came to a little over $550. The basic car, a "runabout," sold for $750, which left a profit of about $200 on each car sold.

The car itself, called the Model A, was lighter in weight than most cars then produced. It weighed about 1250 pounds and was powered by a two-cylinder engine. The little engine developed eight horsepower and could run the car at speeds up to thirty miles per hour. The car had no door, no running board, and though it stood high above the street, had only a six-foot wheelbase. At extra cost, a "tonneau"—a detachable rear seat—was available to the customer.

In the beginning, the company employed only a dozen or so workmen who received salaries of $1.50 per day. As the parts arrived and were dumped in several designated spots on the shop floor, the cars were assembled in groups of four. With two or three workmen assigned to each car, first the wheels were attached, then the body—which two men could lift—and then the fenders. Finally the engine was tuned, carburetor adjusted, brakes checked, and the car was painted. By the end of September, over 200 cars had been assembled.

Ford, of course, was put in charge of production. He also had the final say as to design and engineering features of the cars. Always a tireless worker when his enthusiasm was aroused, he spent many, many long hours at the factory. A large amount of his time was necessarily spent in the experimental shop where he worked on new designs and plans. But he made frequent trips through the plant, often taking off his coat to tackle a dirty piece of work or to remedy some problem of production. He had a fondness for practical jokes and in slack moments liked to tell stories and make small talk with the men. In this early stage of the Ford Motor Company, he knew all his employees by name and they all called him Henry or "Hank." He was considerate of his men and they respected him both as an employer and as a man. He never gave orders, but instead hinted that "it would be nice if such and such were done" or "perhaps this could be done soon." His men would take the hints immediately and work with a will to get the job done to his liking.

As to be expected with a new product, there were a few "bugs" in the car that had to be worked out. The radiators, for instance, were inadequate and tended to boil over, even on

a level road and in high gear. The first carburetors proved to be inefficient, the oil pumps defective, the chain drive often gave trouble, and the brake drums sometimes broke. These shortcomings were intolerable to Ford, the perfectionist, and he went to great lengths to make improvements. During the first few months of business, he all but remade the Model A and was later to write, "The cars gained a reputation for standing up."

Of course, Ford's car was not the only one to be born with defects. All cars of the period had their shortcomings, some more serious than Ford's. The art of manufacturing automobiles had not yet reached the stage of mass production. In the very early days, James Packard of Ohio bought a car, (not a Ford), with so many defects that he was prompted to write the maker, "I could build a better one myself!" And he did. The Packard car, which no doubt had its early defects too, was to enjoy a long and honored place in the saga of the American automobile.

Despite the shortcomings of the first cars produced, the demand, right from the beginning, ran ahead of the supply. Working at a frantic pace, the little company produced and sold over 650 cars by the end of March, 1904, for a net profit of nearly $100,000. It was obvious that they were rapidly outgrowing their little shop. Though another floor had been added, they began to make plans in April, 1904, for a new and much larger plant. Late in that year and in early 1905, the company transferred its operations to the new plant on Piquette Avenue. It was reported to be ten times larger than the old building, and was three stories high. It included a large elevator for carrying materials between floors.

Now the work force could assemble a dozen or more cars at once and the old methods of production were fast becoming obsolete. The operation had a superficial air of efficiency and, of course, any project of Henry Ford's had to be done in a neat and orderly fashion. Still, there were frequent interruptions in the flow of materials and frustrating breakdowns in the continuity of production. It was obvious that new production methods had to be devised. Ford was already pondering the problem.

For awhile, customers purchased cars directly from the factory. As production increased and the company began advertising nationally, it became necessary to acquire dealers in the principal cities of the United States. Los Angeles, New York, Chicago, and Philadelphia were among the first to get dealerships. In Detroit, the company opened a salesroom early in 1904. Foreign distribution followed soon afterward.

Shown at left is an early production scene at Ford's Piquette Avenue plant. By this time, the work force could assemble a dozen or more cars at once and the old methods of production were fast becoming obsolete. The operation had a superficial air of efficiency, but the frequent breakdowns in the continuity of production made it obvious that new methods had to be devised.

LIVERY

Most of the first automobile dealers were men who had previously earned their living in the horse-and-wagon business. Wagon builders, livery stable owners, harness makers, blacksmiths, tire dealers, and even bicycle dealers turned to the new trade. Of course, they knew little or nothing about gasoline engines, and by the summer of 1904 the Ford company began to send out mechanics to instruct the agencies in the maintenance and repair of automobiles. From the very first, Henry Ford believed that service to the customer was of major importance. By the time mechanics arrived to help the agencies with crippled cars, however, they also had to serve as public relations men. Scores of customers with cars that would not run greeted the company representatives with angry words. Most were soon put in good humor as their automobiles were made operable again.

By the fall of 1904, the Model A had given way to an improved version called the Model C. These were also little runabouts and were the lowest priced of the Ford line, costing $850 without a tonneau and $950 with one. The price included two oil side-lamps and a horn. There was also a Model F touring car priced at $1000 and a closed coupe version for $1250. The elite of the Ford line was a $2000 Model B, which Henry Ford never liked but which was produced to satisfy the other stockholders—principally Malcomson.

Early in 1905, Ford and his aides began designing two new models. As a replacement for the Model B, a six-cylinder Model K was planned. This expensive model, weighing about 2000 pounds and costing $2800 was finally introduced in 1906. But Ford himself never had any faith in the large car and when his differences with Malcomson reached a climax, the coal dealer sold his shares of stock to Ford for $175,000. Other stockholders loyal to Malcomson also sold out and left the company. By the fall of 1907, Henry Ford was by far the majority stockholder with 858 shares.

As a result, the way was now clear for Ford to realize his ambition for quantity production of an inexpensive

As Ford production increased and the company began to advertise nationally, it became necessary to acquire dealers in the principal cities of the United States. Most of the first automobile dealers were men who had previously earned their living in the horse-and-wagon business. In this illustration, a livery-stable owner and his helpers are shown hanging a new sign—"Automobiles"—to advertise their new trade.

car. That car, for the time being, took the form of the Model N—the other automobile he had begun designing in 1905. This model, one of the better-made automobiles then produced in America in the low-priced field, was a four-cylinder runabout considerably improved over its predecessors, the Models A and C. The snappy little Model C, first introduced in 1906, was an immediate hit with the public. It was light in weight, (about 1000 pounds), sturdy, fast, (it could reach speeds of 45 miles per hour), and, it was claimed, could get 20 miles per gallon of gas. Ford hoped to market the car for $500, but this proved impossible. The little vehicle finally reached production with a delivery price of $600. Two fancier versions on the same chassis, the Model R, and later the Model S, sold for $750 and $700, respectively.

The stage was now set for the final development of the dream car Henry Ford had envisioned from the very first. The next model, the next letter of the alphabet, would find a niche in history. All the work that had been done before had led toward the goal about to be achieved. In October, 1908, deliveries began of what was to become the most famous car in automobile history—the Model T.

The elite of the Ford line in 1904 was the Model B (opposite, top). In 1906, the Model K (opposite, bottom) replaced the Model B. Ford himself never had any faith in these large, expensive cars, which had been produced to satisfy the other stockholders in the company. His differences with his partner, A. Y. Malcomsen, over this issue caused Malcomsen to leave the company. By the fall of 1907, Ford was the majority stockholder and could begin to realize his ambition for quantity production of an inexpensive car. That car took the form of the Model N (above), a four-cylinder runabout which was one of the better-made automobiles then produced in America in the low-priced field.

The Birth of the Model T

By the year of the Model T—1908—the automobile industry was booming. Ford could now be counted among the "Big Four" leaders along with Buick, Reo, and the Maxwell-Briscoe. In June the Ford workers established a new record. In a ten-hour day, they built 101 automobiles. By the end of the year the schedule called for 100 cars per day on a routine basis, and Ford already was anticipating even greater production. He was now employing over 1300 workers and work was progressing well on a vast new factory at Highland Park. When completed, this factory would be the largest under one roof in Michigan.

In the few years since its birth, the automobile industry had made great technological advances, though by today's standards they were still in a somewhat primitive state. A whole new family of machine tools had come into being. Factories hummed with the noise of automatic screw machines, vertical millers, turret lathes, drills, cutters, hammers, and grinders, many specially designed to do a particular job required in the building of an automobile. If perfect precision had not yet been achieved, at least a solid base was being laid for the development of automobile production as we know it today.

Assembly methods likewise were as yet unrefined. Still, systematic continuity and timing were required to produce even one hundred cars per day.

The photograph at left shows part of one day's production in 1906. In June of 1908, the Ford workers established a new record. In a ten-hour day, they built 101 automobiles. By the end of that year the schedule called for 100 cars per day on a routine basis.

The step-by-step production of the various component parts was closely timed and regulated. Parts placed in converging lines had to arrive at the proper time in the exact place for fitting together. Cranes, hoists, and trolleys were employed to maintain the proper flow of materials. Stocks of other parts were placed at required intervals along the lines of assembly.

At the Piquette Avenue plant, a systematic order of progression began on the ground floor, where the heavy equipment was laid out, continued to the second floor, and then to the top floor, where the car was finally completed and given a coat of paint.

As the factory grew and the number of workers steadily increased, the working atmosphere became less and less personal. Ford himself stayed very busy in his experimental workshop. Occasionally, he made a trip through the shop and stopped to talk briefly with the older employees. On one occasion he is said to have come upon a machine that, though working along with the others, glistened and shone like a silver plate. Ford slapped the hard-working young operator on the back and complimented him on keeping his machine in such fine condition. Henry still had a deep love for anything mechanical and liked to see machines given proper care. The other men in the department noticed his appreciation and a few days later when Ford happened through he was amused to find all the machines shining like the first.

As the company prospered, so did the Ford family. They moved into a new house more befitting the status they had acquired. It was a large house with spacious rooms and quarters for servants. Constructed of red brick with a green tile roof, stone trim, and a porch with stone columns, it had all the modern conveniences of the day. A garage of similar construction was located at the rear.

Clara Ford was delighted with the new house and set out to make the grounds as lovely as the building. With the help of a landscape architect, she put in beautiful gardens, trees, hedges, and lawns. Her confidence in her husband's ability was justified and her heartbreak at leaving the farm so many years ago was forgotten.

Edsel was now nearing fifteen and was enrolled in a preparatory school. His father had built a workshop for him over the garage and he was genuinely interested in mechanics. He also took an increasingly active interest in the Ford Motor Company and even at this early age was given his own Model N runabout.

Thus, in terms of financial security for his family, national recognition, and business success, Ford already had reached his goal. But there remained many plans and dreams for the future—foremost of which was his idea for a "family horse," an automobile for the working man. Now, in the year 1908, his dream was nearly in his grasp. On October 1, deliveries of the first version of the Model T began to reach the public.

The development of the Model T did not come overnight. The research, the successes, the failures, and the total experience of producing the earlier models all contributed to the birth of the new car. The new machine tools, new technology, new production methods, and the discovery of new metals and treatment of metals all helped make the "T" a reality.

One day Ford happened on the scene of an accident involving a French-made automobile. Picking around in the wreckage he discovered a type of metal he had never seen before. The material was very light in weight and seemed unusually tough. Taking a piece back to his assistants, he said, "Find out all about this. This is the kind of material we ought to have in our cars."

After checking with all the leading steel makers in the country, Ford finally had to send to England to get the answer. It proved to be vanadium steel. Ford was quick to recognize its potential and said to an associate, "This means an entirely new design requirement and we can get a better and lighter and cheaper car as a result."

In 1906, Ford had decided that it was time to begin research and development of his new car. On the third floor of the Piquette Avenue plant there was some unused space. Here he had a room built. This was to be his experimental room, and only he and his select engineering group were to be allowed entry.

The room was large enough to accommodate only the full-scale model when completed, a milling machine, a drill press, a blackboard, and a couple of workbenches. For over a year the little group worked almost night and day. Ford sketched his plans on the blackboard and others converted them first to blueprints and then to wooden mock-ups. Actual test parts were made and given trial runs in other cars. Ford himself was not above taking a wrench or another tool in hand and wading in to solve a problem or make an adjustment.

It is true that the invention of the Model T was a group effort. Ford was always weak at reading blueprints and it fell to others in the group to make the precise computations and calculations necessary to a finished plan. But there is no doubt that Ford was the guiding genius. His leadership, his enthusiasm, and his intuitive direction to the project were undoubtedly the paramount contribution. The Model T, beyond any doubt, was Henry Ford's automobile.

The product that emerged from the factory in 1908 introduced to the world many new and ingenious features. It was not a thing of beauty, having been designed more for utility than for looks, but its rather stark and ungraceful lines gave an impression of agility and toughness. The brand new four-cylinder, vertical engine developed some twenty horsepower. The technique of engine-block casting was a major breakthrough in industrial production methods. The detachable cylinder head, a Ford invention, was ridiculed at first but soon became the accepted thing in the automobile industry. Another exciting new feature was the magneto, which was built into the motor to replace the dry-cell batteries used on previous models. The easy-to-use planetary transmission was eagerly awaited by a public long tired of heavy clutches.

The wheelbase of the little car measured only eight feet four inches and the entire vehicle weighed only 1200 pounds. Sitting high above the road, the engine and transmission were completely enclosed. Front and rear wheels were of different sizes, a feature that later caused many complaints from customers. It meant that the owner had to carry double sets of spare tires and tubes.

For the first time, the steering wheel was located on the left. At first the company offered a couple of different colors of paint but within a few months all Model T's appeared in "Brewster Green" with black trimmings and red striping.

Early advertising created a tremendous interest among both dealers and the public at large. One dealer went so far as to lock up the circulars sent out in advance by the company. The customers, he thought, would become too impatient waiting for delivery of the revolutionary new car.

By May of 1909, the company had to suspend taking orders because the production through August already was consumed in advance sales. Henry Ford took special satisfaction in the knowledge that his new car was widely accepted by farmers, who hitherto had demonstrated an intense distrust of the automobile.

For the season October 1, 1908, to September 30, 1909, the Ford Motor Company sold a total of 10,607 automobiles. This was to be the last year for Models R and S. The Model T was offered in six different styles. For $900 in the fall of 1909, customers could have a Model T Roadster. The other styles — Tourabout, Touring Car, Coupe, and Landaulet — were priced slightly higher, with the Town Car top priced at $1200.

With the tremendous sales of 1908-1909, it soon became evident that a more efficient method must be found of getting cars to customers many hundreds of miles away from Detroit. The shipment of fully assembled automobiles was extremely wasteful and a solution had to be found. The answer was in building assembly plants in other cities.

Kansas City, Missouri, was the first such branch factory to be established, at a cost of $30,000. Cars were then shipped disassembled to the new plant in ordinary boxcars at reduced rates. The factory, providing new jobs in the local area and putting company representatives nearer the customer, proved a happy success. Later, other assembly plants were built in St. Louis, Long Island City, Los Angeles, Seattle, Portland, San Francisco, and Manchester, England.

An opportunity to prove the mettle of the little car came early. A New York-to-Seattle race, sponsored by the mining magnate Robert Guggenheim, offered a prize for the fastest time over the 4100 mile route. Two Fords answered the starter's gun on June 1 and rolled westward. They reached St. Louis well ahead of the other competitors.

The lead car, driven by two men named Scott and Smith, plunged on through rain, mud, sand, hailstorms,

---

1908 was the year of the Model T, the automobile Ford had designed for the working man. It was not a thing of beauty, but in June of 1909 Ford had an opportunity to prove its utility. He entered two Model T's in a New York-to-Seattle race. The lead car plunged through rain, mud, sand, hailstorms, and cloudbursts; sank to the hubs in mud (opposite, top); and floundered through four feet of snow in places. In the bottom picture are shown some of the participants in the cross-country race.

Ford

Ford
Ford

and cloudbursts. There were only wagon tracks farther west and they sank to their hubs in quicksand, floundered through four feet of snow in places, and finally slithered down over the treacherous Snoqualmie Pass in Washington, where Henry Ford greeted them. Smith and Scott had made the torturous journey in twenty-two days and fifty-five minutes. The victory was later disavowed because of an infraction of the rules, but as far as the public was concerned, the little "flivver" had proven itself. The winning car traveled down the Pacific Coast and then back to New York before a delighted public.

Mr. Guggenheim gave high praise to the automobile. "Mr. Ford's theory," he said, "that a lightweight car, highly powered for its weight, can go places where heavier cars cannot go, and can beat heavier cars, costing five and six times as much, on the steep hills or bad roads, has been proven. I believe Mr. Ford has the solution of the popular automobile."

Thus, as the first decade of the twentieth century drew to a close, Henry Ford, the Michigan farm boy, had pretty much achieved success in designing and building a car for the average man. Ahead lay the final goal —the mass production of cars for the workingman. To realize this, new methods of production would have to be devised. Greater expansion, on an unheard of scale, had to come. The fruition of his dream required a giant industry and a firm, sure hand to manage it. With faith in himself and in his car, Henry Ford accepted the challenge.

The little Model T "flivver" slithered down over the treacherous Snoqualmie Pass in Washington, where Henry Ford greeted the drivers, Scott and Smith (left). They had made the journey from New York in twenty-two days and fifty-five minutes. Robert Guggenheim, the sponsor of the race, gave high praise to the automobile, and said he believed that Mr. Ford had the solution to the popular automobile.

Something More Than Quantity

Since October 22, 1903, a shadow had hung over the Ford Motor Company in the form of a suit filed against it for the alleged infringement of a patent. For over seven years Henry Ford was to wage an increasingly lonely fight against this attempt at monopoly as his supporters, one by one, surrendered to pressure. When victory finally came on January 9, 1911, the whole automotive world breathed a sigh of relief and Henry Ford became the hero of the day.

A man named George B. Selden had filed an application for a patent on a motorcar of sorts back in 1879. For sixteen years he delayed its issuance but finally, in 1895, he received the patent and four years later transferred its rights to the Columbia and Electric Vehicle Company. The patent was extremely broad and covered no new feature. It simply claimed the invention of a combination of features resulting in a self-propelled motor vehicle which Selden called a "road locomotive."

After 1895, no automobile could be built, sold, or used without Selden's permission. In July of 1900, Selden and the vehicle company filed suit against Alexander Winton—then the leading automobile builder in America. The suit dragged on for nearly three years before Winton surrendered and joined a patent pooling group called the Association of Licensed Automobile Manufacturers. Each of the manufacturers belonging to the group henceforth were required to pay royalties, part of which went to the A.L.A.M., part to the vehicle company, and part to Selden.

Intimidated by the victory of the Columbia and Electric Vehicle Company over Winton, many other manufacturers joined the association. But several independents, led by Henry Ford, refused to give in. The result was a lengthy siege in the courts, with

---

In the photograph opposite, Henry Ford is shown in his office at the Highland Park plant, to which the company had moved at the close of the year 1909.

Mass production is "the focusing upon a manufacturing project of the principles of power, accuracy, economy, system, continuity, speed, and repetition."

a couple of temporary setbacks for Ford along the way, before final victory in 1911. The courts ruled that no one owned exclusive rights to the automobile.

Through the years, Ford had repeated again and again his intention to fight all the way to the Supreme Court and to spend his last dollar to go down fighting if need be. With his decisive victory, Ford overnight became a giant-killer in the eyes of the American public. He was magnanimous toward his old opponent, George Selden, claiming that the old gentleman had fallen into the hands of those who would exploit the industry. In freeing the automobile industry of the threat of monopoly, the Ford company and its individualist leader gained much favorable publicity. Now the road was clear ahead for Henry Ford to set his sights on new methods of production.

No one date in history can be assigned as the birth date of the mass-production system. Indeed, it is difficult to designate even a certain year. But as the Ford Company moved into its new Highland Park plant at the close of the year 1909, its methods of production and its new plant layout showed that advancements had been made along the path to mass production. Revolutionary new methods were to evolve gradually over the next few years in response to the genius of Henry Ford and his dream of making an automobile available to every family in America earning an average wage. By 1913, the year the Sixteenth Amendment to the Constitution (income tax) was adopted, the Ford automobile was being mass-produced.

Mass production is something quite beyond mere quantity production. It is, according to Henry Ford, "the focusing upon a manufacturing project of the principles of power, accuracy, economy, system, continuity, speed and repetition." His statement reflects the total concept, and if any

---

The Ford Motor Company's methods of production and its new Highland Park plant layout showed that advancements had been made along the path to mass production. By 1913, the Ford automobile was being mass-produced. Ford installed heavy ropes and a series of chains and hooks hauled by motors so that parts could be moved along continuously at a convenient height for the men to work (opposite, top). In the picture at the bottom of the page, Ford bodies are shown as they are placed on the chassis. This process was known as the "body drop."

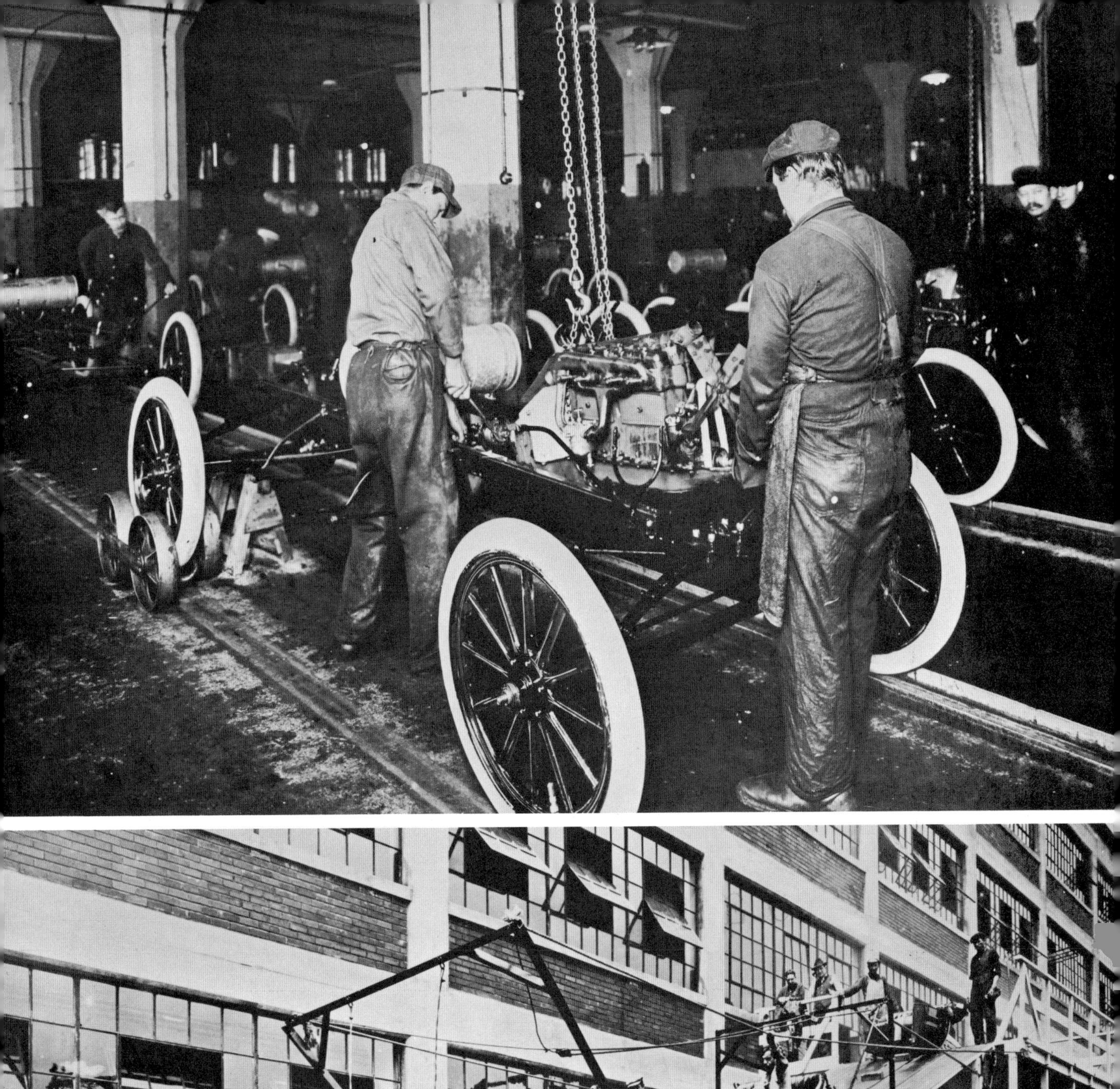

W-1
31
33

one of the elements is missing, the result is something less than mass production.

The basic ingredient still missing from the Ford production lines as the year 1913 began was a moving assembly line—the "continuity" Ford mentioned. The evolution of mass production began with the concept of continuity being applied to the assembly of component parts. For years, Ford and other car builders had followed the same old method. In any given department of the company, each man completely assembled whatever unit his department was responsible for—the magneto or the transmission, for example. If it took, say, thirty operations to assemble the part, each man performed the thirty operations, sent the assembled part to the next department, and began to assemble a new unit. The idea of continuity changed all that.

Under the new system, thirty men each performed only one operation as the part moved past on a trolley or endless belt. Under the old system, each man had a pile of many different pieces of material to assemble; he now had only one. Studies were made to find the best working height, the number of motions required for each job, and the proper speed at which to run the moving line. In a very short time, one man was accomplishing a job in the average time it had taken four men under the old system.

Soon there were several such lines turning out component parts at an ever-increasing rate. All the lines converged at the final assembly department. It was evident that something had to be done to prevent a back-up of completed parts. It was necessary that continuity be brought to the chassis assembly line.

The first approach to the problem was through the use of a heavy rope hauled by a motor with a capstan. The results were gratifying. The man-hours required to assemble each chassis were cut in half. The delighted Ford installed more lines and, applying lessons learned in the parts departments, soon had the chassis moving along on an endless chain at a convenient height for the men to work.

In the months to come, numerous studies had to be made to arrive at the best subdivision of work, the proper speeds for the assembly lines, and the exact timing required to provide precise scheduling of materials and completed parts. The company was soon a dynamic—almost living—thing. As Ford wrote in 1922, "Every piece of work in the shop moves. It may move on hooks on overhead chains going to assembly in the exact order in which the parts are required, it may travel on a moving platform, or it may go by gravity, but the point is that there is no lifting or trucking of anything other than materials."

Mass production in the Ford Company at this time could be likened to a giant river system. In the far-flung corners of the globe, thin rivulets of material—rubber, nickel, iron, leather—began to flow to processing plants. Processed to the needs of the Ford Company, the materials in their new form then began to converge in ever-widening streams at the plant in Highland Park. Over a hundred freight cars of material per day had to be unloaded, sorted, and transferred to the proper departments. Hammered, shaped, drilled, cut, or milled into standardized pieces and parts, the flow was then channeled into the river of final production. Then, in a broad stream of a half-dozen assembly

The photograph at left shows a 1916 production-line scene at a Ford Motor Company plant.

lines, the mighty river of finished products issued forth from the factory sluice gates in the form of shiny, sparkling Model T Fords. As in a delta region, the stream divided once again in its continuous movement to the sea of waiting customers.

The process was fluid, but if a tributary ran dry, the whole precisely regulated system was effectively stopped—as though a giant dam had suddenly been thrown across the mainstream. But when the river was flowing unimpeded, production records fell with increasing regularity and Ford sales rose nearly tenfold during the first few years at the Highland Park factory. By 1917, the year America entered World War I, more than two thousand cars were being produced daily.

Under the new methods developed at the Ford plant, each Model T cost less and less to produce. Back in 1907, Henry Ford had explained to a writer for *Motor World* how quantity alone could bring down the price of a car. "On one part the cost of dyes was $1400. To build one hundred machines would cost $14 each. On the 10,000 we will build it will cost 14 cents each. Work the thing through the whole car and you can get some idea how we are able to do it." By the fall of 1913, Ford was able to market the $500 car he had so long dreamed of. By 1916, the Model T runabout was selling for $345. For the first time, ordinary working Americans could afford to buy an automobile.

As the price of Model T's slipped gradually downward, company profits grew—despite the fact that less profit was realized on each car sold. The very volume of automobiles sold doubled company net income between 1913 and 1917. Handsome stock dividends were being paid regularly, and a large percentage of the profits was being put back into the company to guarantee its growth. New assembly plants were being constructed in strategic locations. New branch agencies were springing up all around the United States and in many foreign countries. The sturdy little "Tin Lizzie" was now a familiar sight in many far-off places around the world. Bangkok, Johannesburg, Buenos Aires, Reykjavik, and Bombay echoed now to the clatter of the Model T.

Perhaps no facet of the Model T's success delighted Henry Ford more than its widespread acceptance by farmers. Riding high above the mud and dust of country roads, undeterred by rocks and stumps, the Ford was a natural on the farm. Farmers as a rule are a practical lot, and they cared not one iota that the Model T lacked the style and refinements offered in many other cars. For all its little faults, the Ford was generally dependable to have around. Farmers immediately found many ways to use the little vehicle as a portable power plant—for hitching to saw rigs, water pumps, and all sorts of farm appliances. The car was cheap, durable, and functional and that was enough to satisfy the farmer.

Though mass-production techniques resulted in tremendous profits for the Ford Company and reduced cost to the customer, there was as yet one man who had been largely forgotten—the worker. With the advent of mass production, the days of the craftsman, in many departments of the factory, were numbered. Where in the past each man assembled a part in its entirety, now he was responsible for only one operation. A job became a monotonous routine requiring little skill, but patience and endurance enough to sit or stand for nine hours each day repeating, a hundred times, the same simple operation. Yet it provided thousands of jobs for people who did not have a trade or special training. Thousands of immigrants, especially many from eastern European countries, thronged to the gates of the plant to apply for jobs that did not require a knowledge of English.

The Ford wages paid in 1913—$2.00 to $2.50 per day—were as good or better than those paid by most industries in the area. But it is typical of Henry Ford that, with great profits building into surpluses, he thought of sharing it with the workers.

By 1917, the Model T was a familiar sight in many far-off places around the world. Above, a big-game hunter uses a Ford on an elephant hunt in India. The sturdy little "Tin Lizzie's" widespread acceptance by farmers delighted Henry Ford. The Model T was a natural on the farm, where it was used in many ways as a portable power plant—for hitching to saw mills (below), water pumps, and other farm appliances.

At a meeting called soon after the New Year began in 1914, Ford sounded out his business associates on a wage increase for the workers. Perhaps he was recalling his own early days as an apprentice mechanic. He insisted on better wages for his workers. A decision was reached, and on January 5, 1914, the company made an announcement that rocked the world. Commencing on the twelfth, the minimum wage at the Ford plant was to be $5.00 for an eight-hour day.

The "Five Dollar Day" was hailed throughout the world with wild enthusiasm and overwhelming praise. The *Michigan Manufacturer and Financial Record* declared it "the most generous stroke of policy between captain of industry and worker that the country has ever seen." Now Henry Ford, already something of an American legend for his swift rise from mechanic to millionaire, became a world hero, a champion of the working man, a philanthropist, and most of all, a man of the people. In the eyes of some, he was comparable to Abraham Lincoln. His frontier upbringing, his homespun mannerisms, his folksiness, fairness, and honesty became legendary almost overnight.

Ford's great fight against the powerful Selden block already had earned him the undying admiration of millions. Now there was more. There were, of course, the inevitable criticisms, but if he did not in truth possess all the virtues accorded him by an admiring public, it must be agreed that he was motivated to no small degree by a deep concern for his fellow man. If he was prompted by selfishness, as his critics claimed, or if he was being unfair to less-prosperous automakers, the undeniable fact remained that he had, in one stroke, doubled the wages of his workers. This in itself was deserving of the high praise and accolades bestowed on him by an admiring world.

The workers themselves, obviously delighted at this unexpected windfall, demonstrated their feelings with increased productivity. A new feeling of pride and comradeship swept the factory. There was a certain prestige now in being recognized as a Ford man and, almost overnight, absenteeism became all but non-existent.

The "Five Dollar Day" was but one of many innovations made by the Ford Company during this period. While the increased wage and shorter hours certainly drew the most attention, such things as better medical care for those injured on the job, extra time for lunch break, and sick leave allowances all contributed to the new *esprit de corps* that swelled in the hearts of the workers. Though increased pressure was applied by the company for a faster pace and greater production, a job at Ford became an enviable distinction.

Henry Ford, perhaps somewhat abashed by the glowing publicity, was later to write, "The payment of five dollars a day for an eight hour day was one of the finest cost-cutting moves we ever made." Despite his attempt to place his motives in the context of good business, the social and humanitarian benefits of his revolutionary plan burned brightly in the hearts of men the world over.

Thus, the year 1914 began with a great step forward in the quest for a better life for all men. It ended, however, with suffering and death making headlines around the world. In the summer of that fateful year, the ancient monarchies of Europe stumbled their way into World War I. Before the year ended, the Germans had been turned back at the gates of Paris, the Russians had been badly mauled in East Prussia, and the British were bombarding the forts of the Dardenelles. Millions of men manned the trenches of the western front and untold thousands rested in newly made graves. The flames of war spread rapidly. The Bismarck Archipelago and New Guinea in the Pacific; the Cameroons and Dar es Salaam in Africa; Tsingtao in China, and many other places around the world soon thundered to the roar of guns and the tread of marching feet. The year that began in peace and hope ended in despair on the battle lines of Europe.

Strikes, such as the one pictured in the illustration at right, didn't occur at Ford plants, mainly because Henry Ford decided in 1914 to pay a minimum wage of five dollars a day—far more than most companies paid at that time. He also gave his employees better medical care, extra time for lunch, and sick-leave allowances. The workers were proud of their jobs, and almost overnight absenteeism became all but nonexistent.

From Pacifist to Belligerent

"I hate war, because war is murder, desolation and destruction." So said Henry Ford in August of 1915. The ever-spreading World War was just now entering its second year, and in the United States a movement was afoot to prepare the military for possible conflict. The sinking of the liner *Lusitania* in May with the loss of 1150 persons, including 114 Americans, had stirred many Americans against Germany and her allies. President Wilson was striving for peace and had succeeded thus far in keeping America out of the war. Despite the preparedness movement, there was a strong pacifist movement in the United States, and few Americans felt more strongly in favor of it than Henry Ford.

In November of 1915, Ford decided to do what he could to help achieve a peace in Europe. At the urgings of Rosika Schwimmer, a Hungarian authoress and lecturer, and others, he offered to put his personal prestige and thousands of dollars behind a peace crusade. Their plan was to solicit the peace efforts of many neutral nations and to set up a commission abroad that would devote itself to "continuous mediation."

The first step was to arrange a meeting with President Wilson, where Ford made an offer to support an official commission until such time as Congress could make an appropriation. While the President assured Ford that he approved of the idea of continuous mediation, he did not feel he could take such a step at that time.

Meanwhile, Ford had chartered a ship to carry a peace delegation abroad and this he offered the President—but to no avail. Ford then said he would take action on his own and went to New York to make arrangements for the sailing.

December 4, 1915, was set as the sailing date for the *Oscar II,* a Scandinavian-American liner Ford had chartered. At a press conference held on November 24, Ford announced that he would assemble a group "of the

biggest and most influential peace advocates in the country, who can get away on this ship." He hoped to attract such notables as former President William H. Taft, John Burroughs, Thomas Edison, John Wanamaker, and many other distinguished Americans. The aim of the expedition, Ford said, was "to get the boys out of the trenches by Christmas." Many of the personages invited were forced to decline in view of the very short time before sailing—nine days. Despite the ridicule heaped upon the expedition by many newspapers, who described Ford as a naive amateur, over 150 delegates, students, newsmen, and photographers sailed from New York several hours behind schedule to the cheers of some 15,000 dockside well-wishers.

While at sea, Ford made considerable use of what he termed "the longest gun in the world"—the wireless. He urged of Congress their support and encouragement for the mission. To rulers of the warring nations he sent messages asking that they try to settle their differences with words instead of bullets. Meanwhile, the liner plowed steadily across the stormy, submarine-infested Atlantic toward its first port of call—Oslo, Norway.

Near the end of the journey, Ford became ill and soon after docking in Oslo he went to a hotel and to bed. Meanwhile, the delegation was holding meetings and conferences seeking support in their quest for peace. Ford, feeling that he had done all he could personally, decided to return to the United States and sailed for New York just before Christmas. The dele-

---

In 1915, the United States was beginning to prepare for the possibility of entering World War I. Henry Ford, a pacifist, chartered a ship to carry a delegation to Europe in quest of peace. At left are snapshots of Ford and his family taken on board the Peace Ship.

gation then pushed on to Stockholm, then to Denmark, and finally to the Hague in Holland. At last a Neutral Conference for Continuous Mediation was set up and Stockholm selected as its headquarters.

If the effort failed in its avowed purpose—to get the boys out of the trenches—at least a permanent group was now established which would devote its energies to seeking peace. The whole affair cost Ford nearly a half-million dollars and even his harshest critics could not attribute the venture to business or moneymaking. Years later, in the holocaust of another World War, the Detroit *Free Press* was to mourn "the disappearance of times when men could still believe in progress in human enlightenment. . . . No peace ship has sailed since the Second World War began. It could find no port either geographically or in the hearts of men."

On April 6, 1917, America entered the war against Germany and, overnight, pacificism was replaced by a patriotic allegiance to the President and to the nation. Henry Ford was among the first to do an abrupt about-face. Later he was to write, "We had, up to the time of the declaration of war, absolutely refused to take war orders from the foreign belligerents . . . it is at variance with our human principles to aid either side in a war in which our country was not involved. These principles had no application once the United States entered the war."

Characteristically, Ford went all the way in his support of the government. "Everything I've got is for the government," he told a Detroit reporter, "and not a cent of profit." All the tremendous assets of the Ford Company were put at the disposal of the country. The great plants and branches, the manpower and the dynamic abilities of the Ford engineering and business executives with their resourcefulness, originality, and productive drive all would make meaningful contributions to the war effort.

By the time of the Armistice on November 11, 1918, the Ford Company had contributed magnificently to the Allied victory. Nearly 40,000 trucks, field cars, and ambulances had been produced, along with such items as artillery caissons, steel helmets, torpedo tubes, and a host of other vital products. For the first time, the company got into the field of aviation. It turned out nearly 4000 twelve-cylinder Liberty aircraft engines. In addition to the complete engines, some 400,000 cylinders for this kind of engine also were produced. For the first time, too, the company had become involved in shipbuilding. The fact that some sixty submarine chasers were launched for the Navy indicates the genius and adaptability of the Ford engineers. To gear up from production of a 1200-pound automobile to a 200-ton ship was a feat few manufacturers would have tried to accomplish. A whole new plant had to be built along the Rouge River to handle the project. The first keel was laid on May 7 and sixty-four days later, on July 10, the hull was successfully launched—a remarkable feat. The tempo of production rapidly increased thereafter as Ford's assembly line techniques were

---

When America did enter the war against Germany in 1917, Henry Ford was among the first to do an abrupt about-face from his pacifism. He went all the way in his support of the government, and put his assets at the disposal of the country. Among many other contributions, the company became involved in shipbuilding in order to build submarine chasers for the Navy (right).

put into action. Boat number fifty-nine was launched just ten days after the keel was laid.

Meanwhile, automobile production dwindled to only 300 units per day and most of these were consigned to the government. After the war, some people demanded that Ford return the war profits as he had promised, even though he was not legally required to do so. No check was ever forthcoming and Ford suffered a new wave of criticism. But it must be said in his defense that he never quibbled over a Federal estimate of any contract and wrote off many millions of dollars that might have been recovered through legal action.

Ford felt, too, that he had incurred heavy losses in potential profits by turning over his plants almost entirely to the government. In the year 1915-1916 the company had realized profits of some $57,000,000. In the war years they dipped to some $20,000,000. Since Ford owned 58½ per cent of the stock in the company, his own estimated loss was in the neighborhood of $22,000,000. Few patriots during the period made such massive contributions to the nation's cause.

Other criticism was directed at Edsel Ford for not having served in the armed forces. He was now secretary of the vast Ford Company, however, and as such was more urgently needed at home. Also, Edsel was now married and a father, facts

Ford had to build a whole new plant along the Rouge River to handle the project of building ships for the Navy (right). The first keel was laid on May 7, 1917, and sixty-four days later, on July 10, the hull was successfully launched. Some sixty submarine chasers were launched by the time the war had ended.

Another major contribution Ford made to the Allied victory came in the form of tractors. Ford had long experimented with the tractor and had built an experimental model in 1908 (opposite, top). By the end of 1917, Ford had built 254 "Fordson" tractors (opposite, bottom). In 1918 the company filled an order from Britain for 6000 tractors. The British used them to grow enough crops to sustain them under the German submarine blockade.

which soon made him exempt from the draft. In November he had married Eleanor Lowthian Clay, a neighborhood girl, and in September of the following year their son, (Henry's first grandchild), Henry Ford II, was born. Edsel, who was twenty-four years old, "wanted to go from the day we declared war," his father stated, "and he wants to now. When the duly authorized authority says his services are more needed in the army than here in these industries, he will be found at the front fighting, and will not be found sticking his spurs into a mahogany desk in Washington." As a writer would later say, it took more courage for Edsel to stay at home and continue his important work than it would have taken to put on a uniform.

Another major contribution to the Allied victory, though not of a military nature, came in the form of tractors. To build an inexpensive tractor that the small farmer could afford, and thus take much of the drudgery out of farming, had long been one of Henry's ambitions. In earlier years he had experimented with the idea, and by 1916 he finally arrived at a suitable model. On July 27, 1917, the Henry Ford & Son Company, (for awhile it would be separate from the Ford Motor Company), was incorporated and, despite a slow start, 254 tractors had been built by the end of the year. With the high seas now controlled to a large extent by German submarines, Britain was unable to import the foodstuffs necessary for its people and the British had placed an order for 6000 "Fordson" tractors. Such were the capabilities of the Fords that the complete order had been filled by April of 1918. That summer found the English countryside echoing to the sound of Fordson tractors as the British worked with a will to grow enough crops to sustain them under the German submarine blockade. The Ford contribution to the Allied cause is an honorable chapter in the company's history.

The Last Quarter Century

Henry Ford's idealism led him to run for election as a United States senator in 1918. He believed he could do some good for the people in Washington. Although he lost, the vote was very close, with his opponent receiving 217,088 votes against Ford's 212,751. It may have been some satisfaction to Ford that the victor, Truman H. Newberry, was subsequently sentenced to two years in prison and a $10,000 fine for conspiracy to violate the Federal Corrupt Practices Act during his primary campaign for nomination.

It was during this first and only foray into politics that Ford came to appreciate fully the power of the press. He soon determined to have a paper of his own in which to express his views. On January 11, 1919, the first issue of his newly purchased Dearborn *Independent* appeared, featuring "Mr. Ford's Own Page" which he used to express his opinions, whims, and wisdom.

Meanwhile the Ford Motor Company, under Henry's guidance, was once again moving ahead with its policy of expansion. In 1915, Ford had purchased some 2000 acres of land along the Rouge River, southeast of his boyhood home. It was on this site that the factory had been built for the construction of the Eagle boats. The land was a low, muddy area but despite its undesirable features, the ensuing years saw the development of Ford's next expansion project—the mighty River Rouge Plant.

With the coming of America's involvement in the war, his plans were temporarily slowed. He also encountered another problem—his minority stockholders, more interested in being paid large dividends, were against spending the huge sums required to expand. Ford solved this problem when in July of 1919 he purchased, for 105 million dollars, all of the stock not then owned by the Ford family. Now nothing stood in the way of his plans and programs. In the meantime, on December 31, 1918, Henry had resigned as president of the Ford Motor Company and his son Edsel was named to fill his place. Henry, however, as major stockholder, retained the final say as to company policy.

On December 31, 1918, Henry Ford resigned as president of the Ford Motor Company and his son Edsel (opposite) was named to fill his place. Henry, however, exercised his right as major stockholder and retained the final say as to company policy.

With the war over and the company firmly in his hands, Ford proceeded rapidly with the vast new complex. First came two huge blast furnaces and coke ovens, then the tractor plant from Dearborn. The river channel meanwhile was widened and deepened, and on July 11, 1923, the first full load of iron ore was delivered into the factory bins.

The vast expansion schemes of Henry Ford were not limited simply to the factory and the Detroit area. In 1920 he acquired huge acreage in the Iron Mountain country of the upper Michigan peninsula. Soon he was in the lumber and iron ore business. In 1923 he added another 400,000 acres including a sawmill, docks, and a town on Lake Superior. Having been concerned at the increasing costs of lumber and ore, he set out to acquire all the raw materials of his own that he would need. As it turned out, he had acquired far more lumber than he could ever use, (wood was fast being replaced by steel in automobiles), and his ore holdings provided only a fraction of his needs.

In the meantime, after being forced to shut down his plants temporarily for lack of coal, he purchased two coal mines in Kentucky and another in West Virginia. In a few years the mines had become so productive that one fourth of the output was being sold to the public. To guarantee shipment of his coal to the factory, Ford soon invested in a tottering railroad called the Detroit, Toledo and Ironton. Much work and repair were needed, but after considerable expenditure, the railway was soon operating at a profit. Ford sold the D.T.&I. just prior to the stock market crash in 1929 for $36,000,000—a little more than seven times what he had paid for it.

Another venture during this expansion period was a shipping line that was in operation by May of 1924. Two six-hundred-foot freighters, called the *Henry Ford II* and the *Benson Ford* for his two grandsons, were two of the largest lake boats then in

After World War I, Henry Ford proceeded rapidly with his expansion plans, which were not limited to the factory and the Detroit area. In 1920 he acquired huge acreage in the Iron Mountain country of the upper Michigan peninsula, and was soon in the lumber and iron ore business. The illustration at left shows an iron mine superstructure.

operation. In all, more than a dozen vessels of different types comprised the fleet, and as with nearly all of Ford's enterprises, were soon making profits.

One exception to the golden Henry Ford touch for making money was his excursion into the field of aviation. Edsel had long been an aviation enthusiast and had even taken a brief fling at building an airplane back in 1910. A Detroit engineer by the name of William B. Stout approached the Fords for support in building an airplane he had designed. After some initial doubts Ford, with his characteristic zeal, decided to take the plunge. The first step was to build an airport, and in 1924 one of the finest airports in the country was completed on Ford property. By 1926, Ford was building a factory to produce aircraft utilizing the production techniques so well proven in the automobile industry. In June of that year the Ford tri-motor was tested before representatives of various airlines. In November the new factory was completed and in 1929 produced eighty-six of the planes that had been nicknamed the "Tin Goose." Soon after his famous solo crossing of the Atlantic, Charles Lindbergh dropped into Detroit and took Henry for his first airplane ride in the *Spirit of St. Louis.*

Besides the production of aircraft, Ford was also operating air mail routes between Detroit and Chicago and Detroit and Cleveland. In July of 1932, however, Ford got out of the airplane business. Like the "Tin Lizzie," the "Tin Goose" was a durable machine and some were still being flown in America in 1966.

Meanwhile, as the Ford complex spread further and further into many varied fields, production and sales of automobiles, trucks, and tractors rose steadily. From a figure of 530,780 in 1920, the Ford tally passed the million mark in 1921 and in 1923 a high of 2,120,898 was reached—a record that would stand for thirty-two years. In 1922, Ford had acquired the Lincoln Company and was now producing a prestige car as well as the sturdy Model T. But the winds of change were whispering through the automobile industry and the time for development of a better car was near.

For too many months Henry Ford failed to heed the signs of change within the industry. Though his sales remained high, he was steadily losing his great share of the automobile market. He failed to see, or refused to accept, the fact that the days of the Model T were nearly over. Edsel and others in the company were well aware of the fact, but Henry remained in-

---

Henry Ford, in the middle 1920's, made an excursion into the field of aviation. In June of 1926, the Ford tri-motor (opposite, top) was tested. In November the new factory was completed and in 1929 produced eighty-six of the planes that had been nicknamed the "Tin Goose." Soon after his famous solo crossing of the Atlantic, Charles Lindbergh dropped into Detroit and took Henry for his first airplane ride in the Spirit of St. Louis. *Here, the two men stand outside Lindbergh's famous plane (opposite, bottom).*

N9683
Ford
TRI-MOTOR
AMERICAN AIRWAYS
U.S. MAIL

flexible in his contention that the little car had a great future. When sales began to decline in 1925, Henry was convinced that it reflected a lack of initiative on the part of dealers or a poor attitude at the plant itself. He could not conceive that the public wanted anything but utility in an automobile, and certainly the Model T was the most utilitarian of cars.

In late 1925, Henry gave in to some extent and allowed some styling changes to be made. This, and a price reduction, provided temporary results. But in 1926, sales fell off sharply and Ford reluctantly signaled the end of the Model T and the development of a new car. On May 26, 1927, the fifteen-millionth Model T rolled off the assembly lines and Henry was there to greet it and ride away with Edsel at the wheel. When the last Model T rolled out of the plant its number was 15,007,033—the last of the most famous cars the world has even seen.

The changeover, so long in coming, cost Ford about a quarter of a billion dollars. But the new car, called the Model A, was pronounced a success and the response of the public was both gratifying and hopeful. Featuring many innovations, the Model A was quite a superior car to its predecessor. Its selective sliding gear transmission, (Henry had at last agreed to part with the planetary type), was a better working component than that of its competitors. The car was considerably quieter than the Model T, and with a new type of springs and rubber cushions, rode much better. For its price and its day, the Model A was an excellent car. Though Ford had been reluctant to give up the Model T, a delighted public said of the Model A that "Henry's done it again!"

By the time of the Model A, other companies, now using techniques developed by Ford, were threatening to take over as leaders in the automobile industry. General Motors, with its competitive Chevrolet, was running a neck and neck race with Ford for first place, and the Chrysler Corporation, by 1928, was firmly in third. In 1928, Chrysler came out with a low-priced car, the Plymouth, which eventually would compete with Ford and Chevrolet.

Nineteen twenty-nine was the best year for Ford since 1925, with total sales of nearly two million cars. But the depression, following the "crash" of October 29, was beginning to spread throughout the country. The automobile industry began to suffer as the year 1930 rolled around. Total sales for Ford fell to 1,451,574 in 1930 and then plummeted to 395,956 in 1932, the year Ford introduced the first V-8. This entirely new Ford car was to be Henry's last great innovation.

But the country was deep in an economic depression, and people could not afford to buy automobiles. Millions of men walked the streets seeking any kind of job. Soup and bread lines were getting longer and a shadow of despair hung over the nation. But Henry Ford was optimistic and despite his nearly seventy years, he looked for a silver lining beyond the clouds that affected every American. This was the year that Franklin Delano Roosevelt rode into the White House to the tune of "Happy Days Are Here Again!" Immersed in their own problems, Americans cared little in 1932 about the rise of a threatening dictator named Adolf Hitler, far across the Atlantic in Germany. But they undoubtedly took heart when the bright-eyed old man in Detroit told reporters, "I've got my old determination back." If Henry thought things would straighten out, the public would believe him.

But by 1936, the Ford Motor Company had slid to third place in the production of automobiles. The grand old man who had contributed so much to making the automobile industry a giant could not keep up with the times. As the years passed he grew progressively more conservative in his thinking. The old spirit of change was waning. The fires of invention and creativity were beginning to flicker and he became preoccupied with activities other than the production of Ford automobiles. And yet he refused to turn over the reins of the

The last of the famous Model T Fords rolled out of the plant in 1927. The car that took its place was the Model A (opposite), a superior car to the Model T. For its price and day, the Model A was an excellent car.

company to the very capable Edsel who, despite his title of president, still bowed to his father's wishes.

In January of 1936, the Ford Foundation was created. Established to "receive and administer funds for scientific, educational and charitable purposes, all for the public welfare and for no other purpose," it had a modest beginning. Edsel Ford started it off with a gift of $25,000. Eventually the Foundation was to receive the bulk of the Ford wealth and become the greatest institution of its kind in the world, with assets in the billions of dollars.

Well into his seventies, Henry continued to show flashes of the genius that had carried the Ford name to the very top of the industry. But in his seventy-fifth year he suffered a stroke, followed three years later, in 1941, by a more serious one. In May of 1943, Edsel Ford died of cancer and the great Ford plant became all but rudderless. Henry once again took over the presidency despite his age and poor health. His eldest grandson, Henry Ford II, was given a release from the Navy to return to the factory and was soon elected vice-president. In September of 1945, Clara put her foot down and insisted that Henry retire. On September 21, Henry Ford II became president of the company and a fabulous chapter in the history of American industry came to an end.

On April 7, 1947, Henry Ford died in his bed at his home in Dearborn. Because of a flood, the power had failed, and with it the heat, electricity, and telephone. Thus, in his final moments, the great genius of modern industry and mechanical invention lay in the light of an oil lamp and flickering candles, warmed only by the heat of a wood fire. After a lifetime dedicated to progress, Henry Ford died under conditions little different from those at the time of his birth.

On April 7, 1947, Henry Ford died in his bed at his home in Dearborn. He was buried in the family cemetery at Dearborn, Michigan (right).

FORD

The Legend and the Legacy

For all his greatness, for all his millions, and for all his genius, Henry Ford remained throughout his life a champion of the common man. His life-story, as it unfolded, caught the imagination of the American people. The facts of his grass-roots early years and his subsequent rise to become perhaps the wealthiest man in the world were well known and appreciated by the public. His long, lonely fight against the powerful Selden patent forces won him esteem and applause from Americans, who traditionally cheer for the underdog.

Yet, Ford was always a most controversial figure. Often regarded as some sort of saint, and sometimes considered a devil, his true character is almost impossible to classify. No theory or portrait can capture the whole of Henry Ford. When he cut workdays to eight hours and established the "Five Dollar Day," he acquired a halo. Henceforth, his actions were measured against this aura of sainthood rather than being given a realistic appraisal in the cold light of good business tactics.

Despite his masterful achievements, his character included many frailties and shortcomings. His much publicized benevolence and philanthropy occasionally gave way to a mean streak that seemed to sharpen with his advancing years. He read little and was ignorant in many areas. He sometimes allowed himself to be influenced by the notions and beliefs of other men. Regrettable anti-Semitic statements were made by the Dearborn *Independent.* Ford apologized in 1927 and closed down the paper. He was not a racist, for he employed many Negroes who, incidentally, remained fiercely loyal to Ford when labor disputes arose. For the many foreign immigrants of all nationalities and races, he set up classes in English.

From the very beginning he evidenced a constant concern for the welfare of his employees. In 1914 he established a "Sociological Department" to inquire into the welfare of each of his employees. This innovation had its shortcomings and, of course, reaped more than its share of criti-

In order to obtain privacy, Henry Ford and his family moved from their home to a new and elaborate estate near Dearborn, which they named Fair Lane. The photograph at left, above, shows Ford's tree house on the estate, where he often meditated. Above, right, he sits in a meadow on the estate. The Ford mansion is shown below.

cism, but on the whole it was beneficial. Ford also was among the first to hire the handicapped, and he even provided a company hospital.

For all the many instances of his generosity, Henry Ford never believed in organized charity. He felt it demeaned the individual. Yet he often made embarrassingly generous gifts, such as houses for evicted families. Once he passed some college boys whose old car was stranded by the side of the road. He yelled at them that they should get a horse—but he took their license number and sent them a brand new Model T.

All of his life, Ford was a vigorous man, filled with restless energy and bubbling with new ideas. He seemed to radiate vitality, and those who met him never forgot him. He has been described as having a "slight boyish figure, with thin, long, sure hands, incessantly moving; clean-shaven, the fine skin of his thin face browned golden by the sun . . . and a lofty forehead rising to shiny gray hair like the gray hair of youth; the lower part of his face extraordinarily serene and naive, the upper part immensely alive and keen. He spoke swiftly without raising his voice. . . ."

He was uncomfortable in the company of highly literate men and tended to have only a few close friends. The closest and most notable of these were Thomas Edison, John Burroughs, the naturalist, and Harvey Firestone, the tire manufacturer. The four friends frequently went off on camping trips to the Adirondacks and Alleghenies; occasionally "transient lions" like President Harding would come along.

Ford was uncomfortable in the company of highly literate men and had only a few close friends. The closest and most notable of these were Thomas Edison; John Burroughs, the naturalist; and Harvey Firestone, the tire manufacturer. The four friends took frequent camping trips to the Adirondacks and Alleghenies (below).

"... to build more and more factories, to give as many people as I can a chance to be prosperous ..."

Ford was always a man of simple tastes and had no vanity. Money in itself meant nothing to him and he could never bring himself to spend for luxury and pleasure alone. "I have never known what to do with money after my expenses were paid," he said. "I can't squander it on myself without hurting myself, and nobody wants to do that." In his own words, he reserved nearly all his personal profits for expansion, "to build more and more factories, to give to as many people as I can the chance to be prosperous." Money, he felt, should be kept in continuous circulation. With his mass-production techniques he could produce cars more cheaply. With prices lowered, more people could afford to buy cars. The greater profits realized from a greater volume of sales could be used for expansion, thus creating more jobs, greater production, more profits, and more expansion. The never-ending cycle resulted in more people having a "chance to be prosperous."

With his success and great wealth, Ford soon found himself besieged by crowds of self-seekers in search of jobs, handouts, and charity donations. In the process, the Ford family was virtually driven from their home to a new and elaborate estate near Dearborn, which they named Fair Lane. There, surrounded by walls and guards, the family was at last assured of privacy. In recent years, the house and 215 acres were turned over to the University of Michigan by the Ford Motor Company.

The photograph on the opposite page shows an aerial view of Ford's vast, sprawling Rouge River plant.

For all his great innovations and revolutionary changes, Henry Ford retained a deep affection for the past. In the early nineteen-twenties Ford began developing a monument of Americana at Greenfield Village near Dearborn. From the time of its opening in 1930, over twenty million people have visited this "living history" exhibit where the visitor can take an enchanting step backward in time to experience a few hours of life as it was in the past.

Despite his opinion that "history is bunk as it is taught in the schools," Ford had a deep understanding of the subject. "I deeply admire the men who founded this country," he said, "and I think we ought to know more about them and how they lived and the force and courage they had. Of course we can read about them but . . . the only way to show how our forefathers lived and to bring to mind what kind of people they were is to reconstruct, as nearly as possible, the exact conditions under which they lived." That Ford succeeded in his project is evident to the visitor of Greenfield Village.

The result of Ford's great enterprise is the greatest collection of Americana anywhere in the country. Whole buildings of historic interest were dismantled and shipped to the spot to be reassembled and restored to their original condition. The Logan County, Illinois, courthouse — where Abraham Lincoln first practiced law —is there on the edge of the village green. The whole Menlo Park complex of Thomas Edison is faithfully reconstructed just as it was when the great inventor and his staff were producing the electric light, the phonograph, and the telephone transmitter. Seven carloads of red New Jersey soil were brought to give the place a familiar foundation.

The homes of such famous Americans as George Washington Carver, Noah Webster, Luther Burbank, Ford's own birthplace, and many others are now clustered together in the village. There are old mills and factories, an early printing plant, a carriage shop, a glass factory, and many other reminders of the days before mass production — many with their machinery still operable.

There is one exhibit at Greenfield that is perhaps the most significant of all. It is a little brick shed with unpainted walls and tiny uncurtained windows. There is an orderliness about the shed, with its shelves and crude workbench lined with tools. An old pot-bellied stove, unlit but adding a warmth to the scene, extends its pipe to the opened beamed ceiling. And in the middle of the room is a curious little rubber-tired carriage with a small motor under the seat. This is Henry Ford's workshop, restored to its appearance on the rainy night in June, 1896, when he completed his first horseless carriage.

In was here in this very shop that Henry Ford tinkered over this very machine as Clara sat nearby knitting and keeping him company. If a passerby of that day and age had peeked in the window, he probably would have walked away shaking his head with scorn at the idea of a machine to replace the horse. But had he been able to walk around the corner into the world of today, he would have seen for himself the truth of Henry Ford's visions. The millions of powerful automobiles, and the superhighways that carry them, owe their being to the work accomplished in the tiny brick shed so many years ago. More than any other one single contribution, the genius of Henry Ford put America on wheels.

Two of the most interesting exhibits at Greenfield Village, near Dearborn, are Ford's Highland Park office (opposite, top), where he announced in 1914 the company's revolutionary policy of five dollars a day for eight hours of work, and his original workshop—the brick shed in which he built and tested his first horseless carriage (opposite, bottom).

The avowed goal of Henry Ford, at the turn of the century, was to produce a car the average man could afford. While others scoffed, he pursued his goal with a tenacity and stubborness forged in rural nineteenth-century Michigan. But he dreamed his dreams with a twentieth-century mind, with a rare appreciation of things mechanical. The age of the automobile arrived and the man and the hour met in one of those happy accidents of history that reshape the destiny of the world.

From the genius of Henry Ford came the family car and the revolutionary concept of mass production needed to supply it to the American public. The production techniques devised by Ford catapulted the United States to world leadership in industry. In two world wars those same techniques enabled America to become the "arsenal of democracy."

Henry Ford became a symbol of American industrial ingenuity. He was an individualist with a supreme confidence in himself and his dreams. Within him burned the fires of change and innovation—fires fed and stoked by a limitless energy and a desire to improve the lot of the average American. Despite his great wealth, he retained the Lincolnesque quality of identifying with the common man.

No doubt the automobile age would have progressed without him. But we would be a lot further back along the road had Ford not met his destiny. More than any other man, Henry Ford is responsible for putting America—and indeed the world—on wheels.

From the genius of Henry Ford came the family car and the revolutionary concept of mass production needed to supply it to the American public. The production techniques devised by Ford catapulted the United States to world leadership in industry. Shown at right is one of the most dramatic operations in automobile assembly—"body decking"—where the body is cradled onto the moving chassis. This 1966 Ford plant operation is a considerable improvement over the early Ford "body drop."

Bibliography

*AIRD, HAZEL BLAIR. *Henry Ford, Boy With Ideas.* Indianapolis: Bobbs-Merrill, 1960.

ARNOLD, HORACE LUCIEN, and FAY LEON FAUROTE. *Ford Methods and the Ford Shops.* New York, 1915.

BARRUS, CLARA, *The Life and Letters of John Burroughs.* 2 vols. Boston and New York, 1925.

BENNETT, HARRY HERBERT. *We Never Called Him Henry.* New York: Fawcett Gold Medal Books, 1947.

BONVILLE, FRANK. *What Henry Ford Is Doing.* Seattle, Washington: Bureau of Information, 1920.

BONSON, ALLAN LOWIS. *The New Henry Ford.* New York: Funk & Wagnalls, 1923.

BRADFORD, GAMALEIL. *The Quick and the Dead.* Boston: Houghton-Mifflin, 1931.

BURLINGAME, ROGER. *Henry Ford, A Great Life In Brief.* New York: Knopf, 1954.

———. *Henry Ford.* New York: New American Library (Signet), 1956.

BUSHNELL, SARAH T. *The Truth About Henry Ford.* Chicago: Reilly & Lee Co., 1922.

CALDWELL, CYRIL CASSIDY. *Henry Ford.* London: Bodley Head, 1955.

CLANCY, LOUISE MARKS. *The Believer, the life story of Mrs. Henry Ford.* New York: Coward-McCann, 1960.

COHN, DAVID L. *Combustion On Wheels.* Boston, 1944.

CRISP, J. VAN DEVANTER. *Scrapbook of clippings on Ford's Peace Ship.* Title in ms. at N.Y. Public Library.

CRUDEN, ROBERT L. *The End of the Ford Myth.* N.Y. International Pamphlets. 1932. 15 pages.

DAILEY, BERNARD. "Henry Ford: and the others." *Forum Magazine,* 55 (1916), 313-17.

DUNBURG, BERNARD. "Henry Ford: the Apostle of Peace." *International Magazine,* 10 (1916) 71-75.

ERVIN, SPENCER. *Henry Ford versus Truman Newberry*: the Famous Senate Election Contest. New York: R. R. Smith, 1935.

FAY, CHARLES NORMAN. *Social Justice; the moral of the Henry Ford fortune.* Cambridge, Mass.: The Cosmos Press, 1926.

FIRESTONE, HARVEY S., in collaboration with SAMUEL CROWTHER. *Men and Rubber.* Garden City, 1926.

FORD, HENRY. *The Ford Plan, a human document, report of Henry Ford before the Federal commission on industrial relations 1/22/15.* New York: John R. Anderson Co., 1915.

———. *Peace—Not War.* Detroit: Free Press, 1915.

———. *The Case Against the Little White Slaver* (cigarette habit). Detroit: Free Press, 1916.

———. *Ford Ideals—A selection from his "page" in the Dearborn Independent.* Dearborn, Mich.: Dearborn Publishing Co., 1922.

———and SAMUEL CROWTHER. *My Life and Work.* Garden City, New York: Doubleday, Page & Co., 1923.

———. *365 of Henry Ford's Sayings.* New York: The League-for-a-living, 1923, (film reproduction in N.Y. Public Library) 46 pages.

———. *The Ford Motor Co.—facts about the Ford Motor Co. & subsidiaries.* Detroit: Ford Motor Co., 1924.

———, and MRS. HENRY FORD. *Good Morning (old-fashioned dancing revived).* Detroit: The Dearborn Publishing Co., 1926.

———. *The Story of Mary's Little Lamb As Told By Mary And Her Neighbors And Friends, plus a critical analysis of the poem.* Dearborn, Mich.: The Authors, 1928.

FORD, HENRY. *My Philosophy of Industry* (an authorized interview by Fay Leone Faurote). New York: Coward-McCann, 1929.
——— and SAMUEL CROWTHER. *Edison As I Knew Him.* New York: Comopolitan Book Corp., 1930.
———. *Moving Forward.* Garden City, N. Y.: Doubleday & Doran & Co., 1930.
FORD, HENRY. *The Only Real Security (an interview with Samuel Crowther).* New York: The Chemical Foundation, Inc., 1936.
———. *Things I've Been Thinking About.* New York: F. H. Revell Co., 1936. 32 pages.
———, ed. *Old Favorites From the McGuffey Readers.* New York: American Book Co., 1936.
GARRETT, GARET. *The Wild Wheel.* New York: Pantheon, 1952.
GILBERT, ELEANOR. "A Woman Interviews Henry Ford." *Printers Ink,* 121 (1922), 126-137.
**GILBERT, MIRIAM. *Henry Ford, Maker of the Model T.* Boston: Houghton-Mifflin, 1962.
GLASSOCK, C. B. *The Gasoline Age.* Indianapolis and New York, 1937.
GREENLEAF, WILLIAM. *Monopoly on Wheels.* Henry Ford and the Selden Auto Patent. Detroit: Wayne University Press, 1961.
———. *From These Beginnings.* Detroit: Wayne University Press, 1964.
GRAVES, RALPH HENRY. *The Triumph of an Idea.* Garden City, N Y.: Doubleday, 1934.
HAMILTON, JOSEPH. *Henry Ford, the man, the worker, the citizen.* New York: Henry Holt & Co., 1927.
HENDERSON, ARCHIBALD. *Contemporary Immortals.* New York: D. Appleton & Co., 1930.
Henry Ford: highlights of his life. Dearborn, Michigan: Henry Ford Museum, 1954. 20 pages.
HOLLANDER, STANLEY. *Henry Ford: inventor of the supermarket?* East Lansing, Mich.: Bureau of Business and Economic Research, Graduate School of Business Administration, Michigan State Univ., 1960. 54 pages.
JAMES, ARTHUR. "The Philosophy of Henry Ford." *World Today,* 48 (1926, London), 308-316.
KING, CHARLES BRADY. *Psychic Reminiscences.* Larchmont, N. Y.: The Author, 1935.
LANE, ROSE. *Henry Ford's Own Story.* New York: E. O. Jones, 1917.
LEONARD, JONATHAN NORTON. *The Tragedy of Henry Ford.* New York: G. P. Putnam's Sons, 1932.
LEWIS, DAVID LANIER. *Henry Ford, a study in public relations, 1896-1932.* Ann Arbor, Mich.: University Microfilms, 1959. Microfilm AC-1 # 59-4947.
LOCHNER, LOWIS PAUL. *America's Don Quixote.* London: K. Paul, Trench, Trubner & Co. Ltd., 1924.
LOUREY, HARVEY H. *School Administration* (Fordson schools). Ann Arbor, Michigan: Ann Arbor Press, 1942.
MACMANUS, THEODORE P., and NORMAN BEASLEY. *Men, Money and Motors.* New York and London, 1929.
MARQUIS, SAMUEL SIMPSON. *Henry Ford; an interpretation.* Boston: Little, Brown & Co., 1923.
MERZ, CHARLES. *And Then Came Ford.* Garden City, N. Y.: Doubleday, Doran, 1929.
MILLER, JAMES MARTIN. *The Amazing Story of Henry Ford.* Chicago: M. A. Donahue & Co., 1922.
MOSIER, RICHARD. *Making the American Mind: Social and Moral Ideas in the McGuffey Readers.* New York, 1947.
**NEVINS, ALLAN. *Ford: the times, the man, the company.* New York: Scribner, 1954.
———. *Ford: expansion and challenge 1915-1933.* New York: Scribner, 1957.
———. *Ford: decline and rebirth, 1933-1962.* New York: Scribner, 1963.
*NEYHART, LOUISE ALLBRIGHT. *Henry Ford, Engineer.* Boston Houghton-Mifflin, 1950.
NOBLE, WILLIAM E. "A Student's View of the Ford Expedition." *Mid-West Quarterly,* 3 (1916), 303-329.
**OLSEN, SIDNEY. *Young Henry Ford, the first 40 years.* Detroit: Wayne State University Press, 1963.
PIPP, EDWIN GUSTAV. "The Real Henry Ford." *Pipps Magazine* (Detroit 1922), 218, no. 5.
———. "Henry Ford, both sides of him." *Pipps Magazine* (1926), 216, no. 3.
QUAIFE, MILO M. *The Life of John Wendell Anderson.* Detroit, 1950.
RICHARDS, WILLIAM C. *The Last Billionaire, Henry Ford.* New York: Scribner, 1948.
RUDDIMAN, MARGARET (FORD). "Memories of my brother Henry Ford." *Michigan History* (Sept. 1953), 37, no. 3, 225-275.
**SIMONDS, WILLIAM A. *Henry Ford, Motor Genius.* Garden City, N.Y.: Doubleday, Doran & Co., 1929.
———. *Henry Ford and Greenfield Village.* New York: Frederick Stokes, 1938.
———. *Henry Ford; his life, his work, his genius.* Indianapolis: Bobbs-Merrill, 1943.
———. *Henry Ford, a biography.* London: M. Joseph Ltd., 1946.
SWARD, KEITH THEODORE. *Legend of Henry Ford.* New York: Rhinehart, 1948.
SINCLAIR, UPTON BEALL. *The Flivver King.* Pasadena, Calif.: The Author, 1937.
SORENSON, CHARLES E. *My Forty Years With Ford.* New York: Norton, 1956.
**STERN, PHILIP VAN DOREN. *Tin Lizzie: the story of the fabulous Model-T Ford.* Philadelphia: Chilton & Co., 1955.
STIDGES, WILLIAM LEROY. *Henry Ford, the man and his motives.* New York: George H. Doran Co., 1923.
TRIEN, RALPH WALDO and HENRY FORD. *The Power That Wins.* Indianapolis: Bobbs-Merrill, 1929.
WHITE, LEE STROUT. *Farewell to Model T,* New York, 1936.

*Juvenile
**Pictorial or illustrated
(The New York Public Library and others have biographical information on Ford not separately catalogued.)

Index

Acknowledgments: Photographs on page 2, 15, 22, 30, 63 (bottom), 68 (top), 75, 79, 81 (top left and bottom), 87 (top), and 89 from the files of Wide World Photos, Inc.; photographs on pages 26, 35, 38, 42, 43, 44, 49 (bottom), 50-51, 52, 55, 56, 58, 65, 67, 68 (bottom), 76, 81 (top right), 84 and 87 (bottom) courtesy of the Ford Archives, Henry Ford Museum, Dearborn, Michigan; photographs on pages 49 (top), 63 (top), and 70 courtesy of the Ford Motor Company, Dearborn, Michigan. Illustrations on pages 8-9, 12-13, 18-19, 24-25, 27, 29, 32, 40-41, and 61 by Bob Brunton, Hollis Associates; illustrations on pages 20, 21, 72, and 82-83 by Nita Engle, Hollis Associates; illustrations on pages 11, 13, and 36 by John Hollis.